WEST VANCOUVER STORIES

THE PANDEMIC PROJECT

Edited by LINDY PFEIL

ISBN: 978-0-9813508-4-4

www.lindypfeil.com
www.shongololobooks.com

Shongololo Books gratefully acknowledges that the land on
which we live and work is within the traditional territories of
the Skwxwú7mesh (Squamish), Səĺílwətaʔ/Selilwitulh (Tsleil-
Waututh) and xwməθkwəy̓əm (Musqueam) Nations.

A Message from the Mayor

The pandemic of 20/21 has impacted us all in ways none of us could have imagined. While we are united in fighting this common enemy, how each of us experiences it is unique. And I believe that to develop empathy as a society, we need to hear the stories of others.

That's why the West Vancouver Stories initiative is so important. It's an opportunity for a diverse and courageous cross-section · of our community to share compelling and intimate reflections on life during this extraordinary time; and for the rest of us to understand and appreciate those insights.

To those who contributed to this collection, thank you for opening up your hearts with your stories of hardship, and of resilience; and for reminding us why West Vancouver is such a special place.

I'd like to extend a special note of appreciation to Lindy Pfeil for coming up with this idea, and for working each day to bring people together in kindness. And thank you to the West Vancouver Foundation for providing the funding to make it all possible.

Mary-Ann Booth

Acknowledgements

This book went from conception to completion in just weeks. Twenty-three 'ordinary' West Vancouver citizens, between the ages of 16 and 80-plus, gathered online over the course of three Tuesday evenings. Some had written before; others had only dreamed of writing. We shared our individual experiences of being alive during this astounding time in history. As we wrote, read, listened and learned about each other, friendships were forged. This book is proof that everyone is a storyteller, and that it is our stories that unite us.

I am deeply grateful to everyone who generously – and courageously – participated in this process. I am also grateful to live, work and write on the traditional territories of the Coast Salish peoples. And huge thanks to the West Vancouver Foundation for funding this initiative through their Responsive Neighbourhood Small Grant program.

West Vancouver Stories: The Pandemic Project is a celebration of hope and resilience. It ensures that our stories will never be lost.

Lindy Pfeil

REMEMBERING RUTH

Anne Baird

I spent most of 2020 with my mother, Ruth, though she died 35 years ago. I hadn't thought much about her in recent years. Then, COVID-19 hit. Staying home, staying safe and social distancing were in. I had to realign my life.

I began working on my End-of-Life Book, a project I'd been avoiding. But since I couldn't go anywhere, I decided I might as well tackle it. Mortality's a hot topic these days. I assembled my will, medical preferences and financial information. The *really* challenging part was my Life Story: What I Want to be Remembered For. What cheek! People remember what they want to.

But my friends wouldn't let me off the hook. "Your family won't know about your life unless you tell them. Just *do* it!"

Uh oh. The Nike imperative. Who can shirk that call to action?

I began at the beginning, in Prince Rupert, with my mother, Ruth.

I reflected on her life. Not as the quiet housewife I knew in New York in the 1950s. Nor as the 80-year-old matron who lived in peaceful anonymity in West Vancouver till her death. But as a passionate young woman of 25 who slipped the bonds of Rupert, and set sail for faraway lands and wild adventures with an almost total stranger. Who *was* she? How did she raise three children in some of the most primitive countries in the world? Compared to her isolation in the 1920s, '30s and '40s, mine in 2020 was a romp in the park.

Born in Orangeville, Ontario in 1903, her father, George Alexander Rix, was Bishop of Caledonia, the northernmost Anglican diocese of BC. She led a sheltered life at the manse, planning to teach home economics until she married. After that, she hoped to bring up a fine, Canadian family. A suitable husband was already in her parents' sights.

Instead, in 1928, after a whirlwind, six-month courtship, she married my father, an agnostic Dutch/English petroleum engineer, ironically named *Christian* Breukelman. They met at a tea party.

Ruth was studying domestic science in Victoria, and her Uncle Skipper invited her for tea. Skipper was BC's first ferry boat captain and skippered the ferry from Vancouver to Rupert for years. They weren't actually related, but were family friends. His home was considered a safe house for Mum to visit while in racy Victoria. Dad, who was taking a break from his job as an English roustabout in Long Beach, California's first offshore oil fields, had also been invited for tea.

It was love at first sight. They married, and sailed away to live an extraordinary life in Java, Borneo, Trinidad, Venezuela, and Bogota – before they became tourist destinations.

When Dad retired in 1966, he dreamed of returning to England.

Mum finally said no. "I've followed you all my life. I want to go home to Canada." She'd been away for nearly 40 years.

Prince Rupert was, perhaps, a bridge too far, so they chose West Vancouver. They lived here for twenty years till Mum died in 1985.

In 1997, I followed, emigrating from California. I became a Canadian citizen, and also settled in West Van.

As I walk through COVID-19, I'm inspired by my mother who faced unimaginable challenges in her youth. How did her isolation in those far-off countries compare to mine? I live in one of the most beautiful cities in the world. I have family, friends, and a fine companion. We're able to connect through modern technology. I attend church online and sing in its virtual choir. Thanks to the Internet, Zoom, Facetime and messaging, I never have to be alone unless I choose to be.

Mum's situation was different. She lived in isolation in underdeveloped countries, soon to be ravaged by World War II, or upended by revolution. She didn't speak the local languages. Had no experience in managing households where native servants did everything she'd been trained to do. There were no grocery stores. In Southeast Asia in those days, you grew what you ate, and killed your own meat. She had no social communities to lend her support. Even the animals she loved were different from those she'd cherished in Canada.

Instead of complaining, she adapted. With her gifts for patience and pantomime, she learned to communicate with servants. There were few English-speaking women to socialize with. She never worked outside the home. Never had a vibrant social community beyond it. She applied her

3

domestic arts to sewing clothing for her family, caring for her garden, family and exotic pets. She had a capuchin monkey called Kiss, who wore diapers with a hole cut out for his tail. She adopted Cheepa, a parrot, who woke her every morning by gently pulling her eyelids open. In her high-rise in Switzerland, she trained the gulls who flew above Lake Geneva to feed from her hand. She collected birds and animals. And passed that love on to her children.

Isolation didn't end when she and Dad moved to New York. Though she shared a common language with neighbours, she felt out of place as a woman from Prince Rupert in suburban New York. Shy and modest, she never joined the PTA, couldn't drive, and never boasted of her former adventures. I could weep when I think of the stories that died with her. How I wish I knew them!

In her new isolation in New York, Mum turned again to family, home, garden and animals to fill her life. She adopted eccentric mongrel dogs. Rescued wounded birds by feeding them "rescue remedy," a potent mash of brandy, milk and bread. Many of them got drunk while being rescued, and had to sleep it off in shoeboxes before we released them.

She loved all creatures on earth, except snakes. (Too many close encounters with pythons, anacondas and boas in the tropics.) If one of them was foolhardy enough to stray into her garden, she yelled for Judy, her trusty terrier. Judy pinned down the reptile's head while Mum ran for her cutlass. She chopped the snake into two-inch segments, and dumped them in the compost heap.

"Best fertilizer in the world," she chortled with pleasure. "No chemicals."

As I walk the Seawalk with my memories of Mum, I finally understand her simple secret: she made the most of everything in her life, including trespassing snakes. Her delight in small miracles sustained her. She passed that resilience on to her children. Her qualities have rescued me many times. Never more so than now, in 2020.

Like Mum, I'm focusing on what I *have* and *can* enjoy, instead of mourning what's lost. I cherish home, family and friends. And I cook up a storm, recreating her favourite recipes. She told stories and painted. I write and illustrate stories, celebrating the daily wonders of life that she taught me to see.

I know she'd love my birds. Wild birds. The only pets I'm allowed in my pet-free building. I enjoy the daily company of seagulls, crows, and hummingbirds. Thanks to her memories, and to my End-of-Life project, I feel more alive than ever.

Thanks, Mum. I'm writing my Life Story as I wish you'd written yours. I'll tell your stories as well. The ones I know. You're my model for shutdown. You *never* shut down. Neither will I.

NEW NORMAL

Annie Hill

It's Tuesday morning in early April. I wait nervously in my bedroom – the only room in the house with complete privacy. I'm hosting my first seniors' fitness class on Zoom. I'm uncomfortable with both technology and being in front of a camera. I prop another book under my laptop and fiddle with my screen for the best angle. *Click.* One by one, familiar faces pop up, just like the Brady Bunch. What a relief.

When we went into lockdown to prevent the spread of COVID-19, my fitness classes were cancelled and my clients lost their community hub. For some that was their lifeline. Our province declared a state of emergency closing all schools, non-essential businesses, restaurants and recreation, and imposed strict travel bans. The impact was staggering – nothing to do and nowhere to go.

It has been only three weeks since we were all together in our regular Tuesday morning class, but it seems like a lifetime ago. The on-screen smiles tell me they are as pleased to see me – and each other – as I am to see them. It has taken a lot of preparation to get everyone set up on Zoom, with cameras and microphones working. We meet screen-face to screen-face, confined – but safe – in our homes. We visit, catch up, share stories of friends we have lost. No one mentions the awkwardness of talking over each other as we try taking turns. Then we exercise. That's what brought us together in the first place. Thrilled to reconnect and have something on our calendars, we agree to Zoom again the following week.

My appointment with Wally is entirely different. We agree that it is safe to exercise together, one-on-one, if we meet outside. Safety has new meaning now, but I'm willing to try this and eager to train in person.

Wally greets me in his driveway with a gentle smile. We have met just once before, and only briefly. His blue shirt matches his eyes and his baseball cap makes him look younger than his years. Water bottles, gloves, masks and sanitizer in hand, and we're off!

Wally sets a strong pace as we walk along the empty streets and quiet Ambleside lanes. The wide open space makes it easy to keep the requisite six feet between us, and the warm spring air helps me relax. I exhale.

We transform neighbourhood green space and park benches into our outdoor gym. Despite the extra precautions, and my usual concerns with senior clients (getting injured, falling, over-exertion) our session goes well. On our way home, however, we pass by sports courts, basketball hoops and crosswalk buttons all sealed with yellow caution tape – a reminder that nothing is "normal" right now.

While everyone is feeling the impact of the lockdown, I worry most about our seniors. I'm concerned for both their physical and mental well-being as they spend more time at home in isolation, no longer engaging in their regular activities. Older adults are also scared to leave home. If they contract COVID-19, they have a greater risk of dying. Now, more than ever, finding alternative ways for them to exercise safely and connect with others is essential. There are two options: online or outside.

Throughout spring, I meet my clients on Tuesdays and we slowly adapt to online workouts. As spring turns to summer, I expand my Zoom classes from one to two classes a week. Then three. People join us from the Sunshine Coast and Vancouver Island: my mom, my aunt, my godmother and some close family friends. I start embracing technology – this powerful social tool that I've been so reluctant to use. There's nothing new about what we're doing. Millions of people connect daily through video conferencing and social media platforms. But it's new for us.

My participants adapt well. The distance that separates us begins to disappear. A woman comments on someone else's artwork. She shares the story attached to the painting. A connection.

One day, I arrive home to find a fuchsia orchid on my doorstep, with the message "for your corner." I hadn't noticed that the orchid in the corner of my room had died. But someone else had. There are so many ways to reach out even in isolation.

September marks the reopening of schools, universities, youth sports and my group fitness classes! My children go back to school and I go back to work. I take on three wonderful new clients. My husband, who has been working from home since the pandemic began, has been a constant source of support for all of us. Returning to normal feels within reach.

As the seasons change, Wally and I continue with our walks. Few words are spoken during our hour together, but

I relish this quiet time. We pay close attention to our surroundings, connecting through our activities. I discover two of Wally's summertime loves: soccer and blackberries. Come fall, we opt to be near the sea and work out at Ambleside pier with its breathtaking views.

November brings the usual dreaded rains and soggy park benches and, this year, the second wave of COVID-19. It's growing difficult to keep our spirits up. Just as I wonder if we'll be able to continue through winter, Wally's neighbour offers us his carport for workouts. Touched by this kindness, we accept and adapt to our new shelter, with its sparkly lights and chairs for rest.

What began as a temporary measure to get us through spring has become a mainstay. Wally and I clock over 320,000 steps between April and December and my online classes are going strong. Christmas with family is on Zoom this year, so it's a good thing we've all become experts in technology. As 2020 comes to a close, there are no signs of getting back to our old ways anytime soon. The process of finding our "new normal" continues and I'm so thankful for the support I've had and the friendships I've made while creating mine.

GRANDMOTHERS WHISPER IN THE MOUNTAINS

Brenda Morrison

There were only 30 homes along the still-fresh forest-cut of Stevens Drive. Those homeowners needed the news and, in those days, it came by foot. With his newspapers – the *Province*, the *Sun* and the *Harold News* – slung across his back, my nine-year-old dad looked up from his home in Ambleside towards Grouse Mountain and started walking. He was the very first paper boy in the young British Properties, at a time when mama bears and their cubs still roamed its dense rainforest. One kind homeowner, worried for my fearless young dad, gifted him his dog, Lucky. It was the late 1930s and an acre of land around the rolling grounds of the Capilano golf course, sold for $20.

My dad was a first-generation Canadian, born of Scottish settlers. The only remaining connection with the "old country," Scotland, was my grandmother's piano – a beautiful cherrywood Monington and Weston Iron Cottage Grand. The piano was the pride of the family, who all gathered around as Grandmother played. Its music accompanied my nine-year-old dad, like a warm blanket, as he walked from Ambleside towards Grouse Mountain, Lucky by his side.

Years later, at the top of Stevens Drive, came a new development with a school, Glenmore. That's where dad built our family home, when I was two years old. It was one of a long row of duplexes that ran along the Capilano Watershed, leading to the mighty Capilano River and the grand Cleveland Dam, at the base of Grouse Mountain. I loved to look across the reservoir to the mountains that seemed to go on forever.

There were no fences between the duplexes, just one endless backyard. They were filled with young families, all excited to call Glenmore home. And there were bucketloads of kids. We would find each other climbing trees, falling out of trees, under trees, exploring every inch of that backyard. A seasonal creek ran along the bank. We loved it when the rain came. We would run out to find the creek winding its way down from the mountain, connecting each duplex, whispering "come play."

We were the start of something new and we all felt it. It was a feeling that stayed with us, like the echo of a good song from my grandmother's piano.

Many seeds and trees were planted in Glenmore. My dad and I planted two maple trees in the front yard – one green and one red. I loved to watch those trees as they cycled through the seasons of life. As the trees grew, we did too, in so many ways, as did our imagination, as endless as our backyard.

Our play waxed and waned with the seasons – spring-time ball games, summer sprinklers, fall tree-climbing and winter snow angels.

There was endless snow in the backyard in winter. Piles and piles of it. Enough to build our own snow homes and roll up a few snow friends. One year it snowed for six days and six nights. There was so much snow that there was no getting out of Glenmore, except by foot. All the families gathered to make sure everyone was warm and fed. There was a great sense of community care and belonging.

On Christmas Eve all the families gathered at one home. Santa came every year and each and every one of us got a present, straight from Santa's sack.

As we got older, we wandered deeper and deeper into the forest, right down to the Capilano River, where we made our own dams in the river, stone by stone, and watched in wonder as the salmon swam upstream in the fall. Above us stood Grouse Mountain, ever-watchful over the twists and turns of our adventures. She looked grand with her first coat of snow each winter. And she whispered with the winds that new adventures were coming with each new season.

My bedroom window faced the backyard forest. I looked out that window every night as I went to sleep. Adventure stories came alive as I watched the cedar boughs shifting in the winds. Those adventures wound their way to Grouse Mountain, and beyond. My imagination ran away with me to distant lands, to yet more mountains and valleys with rushing rivers and winding creeks.

Glenmore was home until grade 12, followed by Caulfeild, where Dad built another home, with the help of his family.

The echo of adventure continued with university, celebrating finals by hiking in the snow-covered mountains. Following university, there were more mountains to climb in England, Scotland, California and Australia. The first mountain I climbed in Australia was

Mount Kosciuszko, Australia's humble highest peak. I was a participant on an Outward Bound course and I longed to see the wild brumbies running in the mountains.

Later, I would climb to Gorak Shep, the last village before Everest Base Camp, where I witnessed the start of the world's highest marathon at 5,212 m. As I crossed Chola Pass solo to get to Gorak Shep, I felt the presence of something wise and ancient. The stars – so close – like the echo of my grandmother's piano, wrapped me safely in a blanket of care. I was never alone.

I returned to West Vancouver 20 years later with a husband, two children and a PhD. I was proud that my children were going to school in West Vancouver, just as I had done. And they were going to school with their cousins – a third generation blessed to call West Vancouver home. After so many adventures, life had come full circle. Grouse Mountain was still there, rising from the valley of the Capilano River.

As my children step out of their nest into the world, I yearn for adventure again, new and old. In these COVID times, I long to walk those trails that still wind their way down from Glenmore to the Capilano River. Our home is no longer there. The tall green and red maple trees are gone too. Instead, there are now single, detached homes. And fences, lots of fences. Yet the spirit of Glenmore is still there. I feel it deep inside, grounding me, like the song of my grandmother's piano, echoing the call of home.

And as I look up, Grouse Mountain is still there watching over me.

I am a second-generation settler here on the lands of the Sḵwx̱wú7mesh Peoples. I have learnt a Sḵwx̱wú7mesh word that I cherish – Chenchénstway. It means to lift each other up. That is how it felt to grow up in Glenmore.

As COVID has ticked on, my world has become increasingly small. Like my dad, I have a dog. My constant companion, her name is Rhonda Rhousey. She loves our walks from Glenmore to the Capilano River as much as I do.

What I have come to appreciate in these times of bubbles and physical distancing is that one thing COVID cannot take from me is my relationship with land and place. That inner song of home that echoes in my heart and is grounded in place, as I walk the land, step by step.

As I was finishing this story, I asked a Sḵwx̱wú7mesh knowledge keeper the ancestral name for Grouse Mountain. I was told her name is Grandmother. I breathed that note in with awe and wonder. She has always felt like Grandmother to me, beckoning me home, grounding me.

I am deeply connected to the land that is now called West Vancouver, the traditional unceded land of the Sḵwx̱wú7mesh peoples. As a settler, I am grateful to call this place home, and to walk the land and hear the whispering songs of our grandmothers watching over us.

Chenchénstway.

THIS EMPTINESS

Chris Stringer

I'll be 93 this year and, believe me, I've seen it all. I know I don't get around and people will say that my perspective is narrow but you won't believe what I hear. I have an ear to the ground and to the walls in every nook and cranny of this place, so not much gets by me.

If I was a person, I would be known as a people person. I was built for people and my life has been exhilarating because of it. I have been blessed to share the happiest times in people's lives: weddings, baptisms, Christmases and on. I have been entrusted to share the sad times too where I provide warmth and comfort. However, Sundays are it for me. If Sunday did not exist I don't think I would either.

You've probably guessed that I'm a church. St. Francis-in-the-Wood Church, to be precise, located in lower Caulfeild, an area that was developed by Francis Caulfeild between 1900 and 1930. Building began on me in 1926 with completion at the end of 1927. My official consecration into the Anglican Church of Canada took place on January 1, 1928 so I consider that my birthday. I have never been idle, bored or lonely. Church services have been both orderly and noisy. Bells ring, kids run around, anxious to get to Sunday school, and there is organ or piano music. The choir regales with inspirational anthems and congregations sing so heartily that I've sometimes wondered if my rafters would survive.

I am, of course, a home for spirituality. A place for communicating with God. I'm available 24/7 for people to give thanks and pay their respects, either in congregation or alone.

Just outside my south wall is the Memorial Garden where generations of parishioners' ashes lie. The garden is visited regularly, in summer and winter. People also linger for hours in the meditation centre beside it, overlooking the tranquility of the cove.

In the old days, my hall was hopping with cubs, scouts, guides and brownies. Teenagers would hang out here to play basketball. A few blocks from here, families lived and worked at the cannery. In the 1930s, '40s and '50s, I was *it* for the neighbourhood – the only place for community groups to meet.

Eventually the cannery closed and community centres opened. Two-car families made transporting kids easier. Bus service improved and things became quieter. This was when the smart folks that operate me turned the upstairs Sunday school area into a Montessori School. The secluded back area made for a natural playground. A brightly-coloured tunnel was added, as was a walk-in doll house and lots of sit-on toys. I just love the noise and ruckus.

I am known in Vancouver as the wedding church. Some Saturdays I've hosted three weddings! Funerals can take place any day of the week. The office is open during the week for church business. Daytime groups, like quilters and crafters, meet in the lounge. My evenings are filled with singing, as choirs from all over the community rehearse here.

My hall is busy on summer weekends for wedding receptions and in the winter for community events like dances, concerts, pub nights and fundraisers. These events usually last till around 11 p.m. when volunteers come in to clean so that I'm spotless for the 8 a.m. Sunday service.

I have appeared in movies and TV shows. This involves teams of people everywhere from the cove through the gardens and into the church. Exciting! One year the great Katharine Hepburn performed and the press was uncontrollable.

Life over the past 92 years has fulfilled every dream of a people-oriented place like me. I share people's emotional moments, both happy and sad. The quiet, respectful moments are as inspiring for me as the noisy, exuberant ones. Old and new friends have occupied my life generation after generation. I am the only constant and I love the role I play.

The year 2020 changed it all. For the first time in my life, I experienced emptiness.

When the COVID-19 shutdown occurred in March, church services and facility activities ceased. The Montessori closed in April. My sanctuary, hall, lounge, offices and school sat empty.

Every Thursday, the church ministers, assisted by parishioners, record the week's service. This is broadcast via YouTube at 10 a.m. on Sundays. A few weddings and funerals have been held with very limited attendees and distancing guidelines enforced.

Church leaders took advantage of the situation by giving me a summer sprucing up. On May 25, repairs and painting began! My rotten eight foot high rooftop cross was removed. Birds had been nesting in it. Its 250 pound replacement was raised the 40 feet and installed. In June, my roof was replaced– all 14,682 square feet. It took five weeks. I look good as new again, ready for the next generation's activities.

Life seems to be gradually returning. I am encouraged. The Montessori school opened on September 9 and I love hearing the kids playing again. The church office has also re-opened.

In September, parishioners started up a thrift store called Nifty Thrifty. Volunteers collect donations and prepare them for monthly sales. And in November, a movie shoot brought lights, cameras and so much action. It was so exciting!

Things are far from the norm though and the ultimate 2020 disappointment for me was Christmas. No decorations in the stained glass windows or surrounding the choir. No Christmas tree reaching to the rafters. No carols sung loudly by happy people jammed into every seat.

The Bible says, "Rejoice in hope, be patient in tribulation." So I enter 2021 with patience and hope. Hope for safety, peace and love. Hope that my Sundays return, for without them I might not exist. Hope for an end to this emptiness.

St. Francis-in-the-Wood church portrayed by Chris Stringer.

WASH, RINSE, REPEAT

Deanna Regan

Are we hugging?

We ask each other this in the beginning when we meet outdoors for socially distanced drinks. My friends and I are huggers. I'm not sure when or why it started, but it's as automatic and cherished as my morning coffee. Not hugging feels alien and rude. In the first confusing weeks, when we had to rethink every task, from grocery shopping to going to work, we grew weary from so many adjustments. We threw in the towel and embraced, flagrantly breaking the rules, unwilling to relinquish the hugging tradition for a select few. Those early outlawed hugs felt like standing up to the bully on the playground – brave and good and a little bit scary.

It's been months since I've come within a few feet of anyone outside my family. Since then the word cancelled has been thrown around more than the term *new normal*: jobs, classes, lessons, trips, graduations, parties – all cancelled. Also included by extension is mental health, hopes, dreams, lives. We are united by the cancellation of 2020. Events and dates once circled in red on calendars quietly tick by, unnoticed.

Snapping the elastic loop behind my ears and fitting the cotton mask snug around my nose so no droplets can escape, I think I might suffocate if the coronavirus doesn't take me down first. A memory flashes by, of a plastic Minnie Mouse Halloween mask that I wore when I was eight, with a tiny, insufficient hole for oxygen. Between the plexiglass barrier and my mask-muffled speech, ordering deli meat at the grocery store becomes an adventure in pantomime. I realize how much I relied on the lost art of lip reading now that mouths are hidden behind cloth.

I drive to work on deserted streets, and slow down as a crow hops lazily across the intersection of Fifteenth Street and Fulton. The mornings I battled school traffic and impatient commuters are gone. Just the odd dog walker, a few runners, and birds rule the pavement. Rush hour is also cancelled, which is not terrible. Work doesn't provide an escape. All day I deal with COVID-related problems. But it's a change from the banality of waiting for Dr. Bonnie Henry's next announcement.

My key opens the door that used to fly open automatically when I stepped within a meter of it. I still fumble with the key, months into the pandemic. The skin on my hands is parched and raw from the combination of hand washing and sanitizer dispensed from plastic stands that have become as ubiquitous as Walmart greeters. I close the door behind me, ensuring the dead bolt clicks back in place, and walk past an empty gymnasium, lights off, wooden floor glistening with fresh wax.

Once safely in my office I remove my mask, sanitize my desk that already gleams, and catch up on breaking news that will direct my day and affect our programs.

Part of my work these pandemic days is doing community outreach calls to seniors. They answer the phone cautiously, expecting some sort of scam, but drop their guard when they understand I'm calling to make sure they're okay, to see if they are getting the food they need and if they have friends and family helping them through the pandemic. Some report they are thriving, connecting with friends on the phone, learning to order groceries online, having Zoom calls with their choir, and sewing masks. Others cling to my voice like a lifeline, telling me stories of their childhood or experiences during the Second World War. The coronavirus is much worse, one woman explains, because during wartime you could see the missiles and the enemy, but this virus is invisible and potentially everywhere at all times, with no respite. I speak with a high risk senior afraid to leave her apartment, a man in his eighties caring for his wife with dementia who has stopped eating the meals he can prepare, a widower whose wife died from a long illness with cancer and he can't hold her funeral. They are sad, lonely and afraid. My offerings of empathy and advice on how to access services seem like paltry crumbs.

The stories and conversations stay with me as I pack up my empty food containers at the end of the day – I pack lunches daily since the cafe is closed. This virus throttles the weak and lonely, while others skate through virtually unaffected. My family is not bereft because of the pandemic, but neither are we totally immune to its tentacles. I try to bury the guilt I feel for being on the luckier side.

I make my way back home on quiet streets, wondering how the residents of each Ambleside home are faring as I pass the eclectic combination of old homes and new. As I open my door a tiny brown ball of fur springs to life in an enthusiastic salute. Our puppy arrived March 3, when toilet paper hoarding was in its infancy, and talk of a virus shutting down China was as far away as the Arab Spring. Our cavapoo, a cavalier mixed with poodle which when combined renders a living teddy bear, has us walking streets and alleys, meeting neighbours and dog owners daily. Without any notion of social distancing, she charges towards pedestrians as though they are chicken bones. Some dog walkers ask if they can pet her, while others cross the street and avoid eye contact. I have no idea what social isolation feels like, I have never met more people. And so, it is the worst of times, yet in other ways it is the best of times. I say the second part quietly, in a whisper, and only to myself. To say that publicly would be wildly insensitive. It is the best of times so long as the virus keeps its distance from friends and family.

As I rub my puppy's tummy, raised voices debate who used the last of the almond milk and put the empty container back in the fridge. My two oldest came home early from university, their summer jobs cancelled, and are finishing courses online. Our family together again – unexpectedly soon – is the best of times. Spirited discussions on what to make for dinner and how long it takes to disinfect groceries battle for airtime above CBC radio as they walk around the house, their laptops open, perched in the palm of one hand while they wave the other to make their point. The bedroom door of my youngest daughter, still in high school, is closed against the din. She vigilantly sits at her desk attending Zoom classes from 8:30 a.m. to 3 p.m., faithful to her pre-pandemic schedule.

Mild irritation aside, it seems fine. Yet mental health issues were planted by the sudden social isolation, fed and watered throughout the summer as restrictions continued. We are fortunate: we have each other, our health, our puppy, jobs and school to occupy us, and we catch up with friends on hikes. But silently and slowly, in the same way

24

infected droplets unknowingly pass from one to another, the virus attacks us in different ways. A constant discussion takes place around how my children can see their friends safely. It becomes apparent there is a blurred line between following the public health orders and mental health: pick your poison, COVID-19 or depression? Our step counts soar as we walk and talk to connect with friends, and cling to the bits of connection we can safely manage.

Lacing up my runners, I head to a nearby trail. There is a cardboard cutout of a large cougar at the trailhead with a reminder to please remain two meters apart, roughly the length of the cougar. Normally I have the trail to myself at dinner time, but today it's packed with walkers. A man dives into the bushes, turning away from me, burying his mouth and nose in his jacket, as I trot past him. I feel a mixture of guilt for being there and anger that he feels the need to protect himself from me in such an obvious way. The days of smiling and saying hello to passersby are also cancelled.

I recall the words of the sweet senior I spoke with, the one with the proper British accent. She told me about the war sirens that would alert them to go to the bunker, and how they would huddle together and wait for the bombers to finish their nightly attack. It was so much friendlier. Neighbours, friends and strangers helped each other. What makes this virus so devastating and brutal, she said, is it forces us into isolation to fend for ourselves.

By the time I get back home from my run, my daughters have set the table, and my partner has cooked a vegan meal to please everyone but himself. We sit down to our 65th consecutive home cooked meal in our dining room. (There will be hundreds more.) Tomorrow I'll wake up and do it all again, to a slightly different soundtrack.

Wash hands, air dry and repeat.

THE WINDS OF COVID-19: A EULOGY

D. Higgins

The advice I did not follow until seven years later, was to document my feelings after my father died in 2013. My daughter proposed the idea of a journal because she knew that my grief would need an outlet. Ironic that the journal is a travel diary, and fitting that my father's spirit lingers in these words.

We are in our tenth month of COVID-19 restrictions and the similarities I have been drawing with war are haunting. Rationing food, being limited to when and how we shop, wearing masks, hunkering down, worried about what's next – will it get worse or better? Being tied to the radio or laptop for the latest news and zoning in on family and survival. There is, though, one major exception – and this is when things got really grim – the 'no hugging' rule. There is so much back-and-forth love in a daughter's hug.

My father was 11 years old at the beginning of World War II. Wherever he walked in his home of Manchester, UK, he was unsafe. In 1940, over 400 tons of bombs were dropped on his hometown by German bombers, an event that was later called the Christmas Blitz. Brits were not safe in their own homes and were advised to build bomb shelters. Dad dreaded having to spend time in the shelter in his front yard. It was cold, damp and dark. Sirens sounded when air raids were imminent and the family would rush to the shelter ladder in panic, wondering if they would make it in time.

At one point my grandfather, Daniel Leo, was returning home from his shift patrolling for Air Raid Precautions when a nearby explosion propelled him down the ladder and into the shelter! Uncles and fiancés of aunts were sent to France as soldiers and were never seen again.

My father once told me of the terrible time when he and his younger sister, Pauline, were put on trains to live with distant relatives – in separate households – in the country. Recalling the events, his voice caught for a second before returning to its usual jovial tone. He would have preferred to stay with his family in the war zone.

While the bomb shelter was dark and foreboding during the war, in COVID-19 the darkness lingers in the light. The virus floats freely over mountains, crossing international borders in an invisibility cloak, at all times of the day and night. Unlike the bombs of wartime, our current danger is neither seen nor heard. Instead, it occupies the air and floats on the wind searching for new hosts.

Since March of 2020 we have not let our guard down. How can we, when our enemy is invisible? No warning sirens, no noise from bombers flying overhead, no fires from explosions, just the constant possibility that we are inhaling the virus.

In times of duress during this pandemic, I tell myself, 'at least we don't have bombs falling on us. If we stay home we can be safe.' Perspective is my anchor and remembering scenes from my father's childhood helps me stay the course. It gives me the strength to get through it. His history is my present-day gift. Part of me is relieved that my father is not one of the many elderly souls enduring a solitary hell. Yet, another part of me longs for his gentle, reassuring voice.

I miss the way he used to pronounce my name in his lilting, Northern England accent. I miss the possibility of his laugher right around the corner. I miss the comfort that only he could give his eldest daughter in times of sadness. I miss his unconditional love.

I long to ask my father about his youth in wartime and his thoughts about the current world situation. What were his fears at the time? Nobody knows how long we will be living in these conditions and nobody knew World War II would continue for six long years.

My father and his friends attended school for half days because the air raid shelters only had capacity for half the school. When school was not in session, Dad had a band of friends with whom he would roam in the forest, rivers and fields. They built rafts. They rummaged around outside, collecting jagged pieces of metal from artillery, enjoying the danger and freedom that comes from unsupervised and unstructured times. Tough times created tight bonds, and vivid, lasting memories. Dad's friends stayed in touch for over 60 years despite two of them immigrating to Canada.

What will be the bonds that COVID-19 creates?

Could it be that one bond is a virtual presence of a spirit, animated by a look or a gesture? The spirit may be our common understanding that we are living in a kind of war. Our common goal is to vanquish the virus and survive.

This pandemic, like World War II, is becoming an integral part of our autobiography.

I wish I knew for sure if my father's way of dealing with life events was intricately related to his experience as a boy in wartime UK. As he navigated future tragedies, I imagine his point of reference was the war. Although his emotions were tucked away in his ledger, like most men of his generation, his resolve to carry on like a soldier in life was a beacon for me as a young woman.

Thank you, Dad, for your strength and resolve as I navigate COVID-19, accompanied by memories of your beautiful voice recalling stories of a young boy growing up in wartime.

AN IRRITATING GRAIN OF SAND

Domenica Mastromatteo

Stop. Gather the children and the dog. Hold the space. And wait. Just wait.

My life was finally back on track. After years of shedding all that I didn't like – material possessions, unhealthy relationships, outdated ideas and beliefs – I was finally on solid ground and ready to move forward. I had done the hard work of deconstruction and was putting myself back together. I felt good enough and secure in my simple life with my three children in a rented West Vancouver home, a safe space for all of us to rediscover ourselves. We had sheltered in place and were finally ready to move forward.

I had gone back to school in September 2019 to become an art therapist, pursuing my passions of reading, writing and making art at the Vancouver Art Therapy Institute. I was learning and practicing and loving every bit of it and then it all stopped. Time, again, to shelter in place.

My dog, Bonnie, lies beside me on her pillow as I write, exhausted from our walk this morning. While exploring the rocky beach at Ambleside's dog park, I found an open oyster, its pearly interior displayed. I brought it home as both a souvenir and a testament to nature's brilliance. The pearl-making process is a reminder that we are capable of emulating this healing transformation.

When a grain of sand enters the shell, the oyster secretes its healing substance around the grain. Layer upon layer, the pearl is formed. Within the safety of the oyster, the irritant is transformed into something beautiful. As we're asked to shelter in place again, I think of how this unwelcome news can be a source of inspiration for all of us to keep growing as individuals. How do we turn this irritating situation into a beautiful pearl?

Sheltering in place is familiar to me. My life has changed many times, and each time the shelter in place became a transformational process. I embraced the emotional pain, so common during times of change, treating it like a grain of sand. I accepted it, embraced it and watched it evolve into something new.

I love staying home with my children. I love quiet time with nothing to do. That's when the magic happens. As everyone tries to find their way out of boredom, I retreat to doing nothing and letting the magic unfold.

My art therapy training continued with reading, writing and art making. I was able to move my practicum online. With a desire to serve my community during this difficult time, I developed a telehealth art therapy group for adolescents and young adults. The group is a regular stabilizing presence in this new world of worry and uncertainty due to the COVID-19 pandemic. I am a fellow traveller and learn along with them.

Like a container, my art therapy space holds feelings and experiences. As we work on issues of isolation, fear and anxiety, we honour the painful disharmonies of life. I have learned that I am a confident leader, able to create a space of psychological safety. Working with them, I witness the importance of being in community.

Bonnie stirs beside me, reminding me again that I am not alone. I have always wanted a dog. But COVID-19 finally gifted me the time I needed to stay home and care for a puppy.

Art therapy too has made my process through this pandemic interesting and life changing. Making art helps me to acknowledge and make sense of my wounds. It allows me to remember myself and put the bits and pieces of my life together in a way that makes sense for my family. I share this restorative process with my clients, continuously learning as I witness transformations.

My home, my shelter, my space is the inside of the oyster. Art therapy is the process that transforms that irritant grain of sand, coating it layer upon layer into an iridescent pearl. My role is to hold that empathic space of hope, enabling people to move through their own process of healing and self-discovery, to become more fully integrated.

Weeks turn into months. Time passes. Everything stays the same. We wait.

EMBRACE

Elizabeth Wooding

I wondered what it meant: how could two broken people share one heart? I gazed at the sculpture, intrigued and confused. There they were – broken fragments of rusty iron. Two bodies collapsed on one another. Each propped up only by the other's broken pieces. And yet, through the rust and tangled metal, through the confusion of their bodies, I saw ... there ... in the middle ... a single red heart. Was it beating? I reached out to touch it. Was it ...

"Hope?"

The vacuum whirs.

Blinking, fingers outstretched, I find myself staring down at a red ball of dust lodged in the bristles of the vacuum.

"Ha! There's none of that." I pull the red fluff from the vacuum, flip the lid to the garbage can and gruffly toss it in. "How can there be hope if there's no love?" The can slams shut, the clank echoing with steely finality. I shudder and my mind takes me back in time.

There was a lot of silence back then. Funny how naïve we were. It was all a silent game. We thought we were the players and that the pieces were in our control. But it was no game. There were no rules. There was no board to play on. We were the pieces – in free fall. Broken pieces.

The weight of the thought wakes me from my reverie as I collide with the laundry room door. "Shit." The basket of dirty clothes on my hip sways and I tighten my grip. I yank at the door. It's stuck, caught in a broken frame.

"Everything is broken around here!" Frustrated, I tug harder. The door groans under my efforts and reluctantly gives way, leaving me wedged between it and the broken frame.

Angry now, I yell at the door. "I am stuck and broken, living with a man who is stuck and broken!"

And then I feel it in my heart. A flutter? No, a tremor. It's barely perceptible, tiny and tremulous. My breath shallows. The tremor spreads down my arms and into my fingertips. My chest tightens. I know this feeling: worry is setting in.

It's March 2020. COVID comes and he moves into the spare room.

"Precautions."

"Of course."

April. May. I worry. I shake.

June. July. August. I worry. I work.

September. October. November. In my room. Alone. Awake. I worry. My muscles twitch. Micro spasms migrate across my body, jumping at random from one muscle to the next.

"What is happening to me?"

The worry spreads across my body – again. It's 3 a.m. and I can't sleep. It's been months of not sleeping. Am I getting sick? My mind is spinning.

So many questions. "Is this what I want? Will this be how it goes? Am I really going to worry and shake here alone in the dark all night – again?"

I think of the sculpture: the broken embrace. I see them holding each other – face to face.

"Can I face this?"

I make my decision, and in a moment the covers are off and I'm padding down the stairs.

It's quiet in his room. Standing beside him, I break the silence and whisper his name. He startles awake. I hold my breath. Eyes soft and sleepy, and a little surprised, he smiles and lifts the cover to invite me in. The bed is warm. He is warm. I rest in the quiet intimacy and exhale. He pulls me close and I feel the heat of his skin on mine.

Nuzzling in, he whispers, "What's up?"

His breath is warm and soothing. I feel better just being in his arms. I breathe. The iron rods that are my nerves soften. I tell him about my worries. He listens and asks questions. We talk. He reassures me. Holds me. The tremor in my heart eases, my muscles calm and hours pass. I still can't sleep but I am feeling safe, and …

"Loved." The word escapes in a whisper. Astonished, I pause to breathe it in.

My mind slows. "It's soft here."

His arms envelop me and he tells me how he would like to be close again. He'd like to hold me, for us to hold each other, feel each other. "It's been a long time."

Listening, I breathe, feeling safe, calm – loved. We fall asleep as the soft morning light peeks into the room.

What shifts I can't really say. It is both subtle and huge. His caresses – so gentle.

"This feels new." Something inside me comes to life. Something I thought I had lost forever tingles under his touch. "Can I do this?" My back to him, his gentle caresses call to me.

Inhaling deeply, I turn toward him and lay my body the length of his. Warm, soft, electric. We move together, delighting in each other's scent and touch. Falling into sensation, melting into the feel of him. Sensing emotion, tenderness, love, we collapse in each other's arms, tears falling.

"I love you," he says.

"We've been through so much."

In that moment I understand how it is that, once broken, together we share one heart.

SO MUCH RIGHT NOW IS UNKNOWN

Elke Babicki

December 20, 2020

My Darling Eve,

Since we live oceans apart, I am looking at a baby photo of you while writing this letter. You have such an open smile and inquisitive eyes. As it is my profession to understand people's minds, I cannot help but wonder how you are seeing the world now – a year after this photo was taken – with a much-feared virus impacting the world and the people around you.

Has it affected you that your parents' faces are frequently hidden behind masks and you cannot read their expressions? Do you sense through them that the world has become a scary place? When adults struggle, so do their children. As parents' anxiety increases, it often manifests even more in their children.

What kind of repercussions will there be in the long run from people's anxiety over losing their jobs and businesses, not getting medical procedures, not connecting to their families? There are very few studies yet on how people are dealing with the stresses and uncertainties of COVID-19 and the intensified anxiety that has followed.

Fortunately, as anxiety in humans increases, often their resilience increases as well. Humans are remarkably adaptable, Eve. Resilience is that wonderful term for something that helps you persevere through hard times. We develop coping mechanisms that protect us, like immunity to certain diseases.

When I was about eleven years old, I came down with a bad case of German Measles. Our family doctor visited me at home. My temperature was very high, and the red bumps covering every inch of my body had been getting worse. I was aching, itching and listless. The doctor held my hand and talked to me. I do not remember him doing much, besides giving me pills to relieve the pain and reduce the fever. But I have never forgotten the human connection. His care gave me hope that things would get better.

Serious illness was almost a certainty in those days. My father Alex, your grand-uncle, spent five years in concentration camps as a teenager before making his escape just before the war ended. During his confinement, he experienced the worst diseases imaginable. He suffered from typhus and diphtheria, with no amenities like bathrooms or soft beds or even medication. Miraculously, he survived. He walked away a 20-year-old shadow of his former self.

Our family has resilience in spades, dear Eve. My father was a tough kid. His self-reliance and stubbornness served him well in carving out a new life. But it also fused him like molten armour. It made him hypervigilant, intensely driven, preoccupied with safety, and terrified to be vulnerable. When people cope by armouring themselves, it can end up hindering them later. Their road in life becomes narrower, more fenced-in and claustrophobic. It is my hope for you Eve, that you feel safe enough to trust people and that you travel a wide road of possibilities, without many fears.

My own resilience showed up many times over the years, but never more so than during a recent trip to Africa. I was driving through grasslands in an open jeep in northern Botswana, with a guide. It was early morning – the ideal time to see the predators of the night make their way to their sleeping places.

"The lions should be no problem to find; we are constantly coming across them," the guide said, as she drove. "But if you're really lucky, we may see a leopard."

Luck was in our favour that day, Eve. The guide suddenly veered off the main road, hitting the gas until we reached the rare animal she had spotted. Then she cut the engine. We knew to stand still and remain quiet.

The leopard did not, as I expected, retreat. Instead, he moved silently and gracefully towards us with his impressive paws. His spotted fur shone in the sun. With every move, his muscles rippled under his skin.

I was on the top step of the small ladder used to exit the jeep. The leopard was heading straight for me. I remained glued to my spot while he approached steadily. When he was directly beneath me, our eyes met. His black pupils, wrapped in light green translucence, looked almost human.

Though the leopard could easily have attacked me, I was not afraid.

And then he changed direction and trotted quietly away. He climbed a tree and disappeared. It all seemed to happen in slow motion.

"In the wild, there are only three possibilities," our guide said. "You move on, you adapt, or you die." She was talking about the leopard's ability to escape certain death by its predator, the lion, but I felt she was talking about us, too. In the open jeep, staying as silent as possible, we had adapted, so that the leopard wouldn't jump.

When we are faced with that kind of experience, there is no time for fear. Only the moment exists. And in that moment, you know what to do for your best chance of survival. The simplest things in nature, totally primitive and instinctive, can explain so many complicated things, can't they Eve? It really is all about one thing: survival.

In that moment of facing the leopard, the world stopped. It feels much the same way now as I stare into the eyes of this virus taking over the world.

I am reassured by the measures we are taking. We wash our hands regularly and wear masks to protect others and ourselves. This decreases anxiety about spreading the virus. Of course, we do not know how history will look back upon this time. How people's minds, their businesses and the economy will be affected, is uncertain.

I try to be discerning about all the information I receive daily and I don't believe every popular trend designed to provoke fear. Remember FEAR, Eve, as False Evidence Appearing Real and don't let yourself be deterred by it. When in doubt, ask yourself if what you have been told is really true and if the contrary could be true as well. Do your own research and gather your own evidence. Rely on your own intelligence Eve. Listen, evaluate, speak with kindness, but speak up when needed.

When I think of my father as a fifteen-year-old, the image of a juvenile leopard ripped from his family springs to mind. Taken from all he once knew, kept in a small cage, he is unable to roam, play, hunt, or grow into adulthood in his own way. If, after years of deprivation, a leopard is able to leave his cage and adapt in the wild, I do believe anything is possible. And, when I look at this picture of you, dear Eve, with your smiling face and innocent baby eyes, I am reminded of just how great the possibilities are. The human race is remarkably resilient and even if the stability of the world is eroded now, we will adapt again. And so will you.

With love always,
Your Great-Aunt Elke

AN ARTIST IS BORN AND A BLOSSOM FLOURISHES

Fay Mehr

"When I look at you my heart aches," Parvaneh said, sitting across from me. It was a rainy afternoon in 1986 and we were meeting secretly for tea on a busy street in central Tehran.

"What do you mean?" I asked her.

"You were a little blossom that was going to thrive and flourish into a beautiful happy person with a zest for life," she said sadly. "But before it had a chance, it withered, and that hurts my heart."

We sat in silence, mourning.

I was sixteen when I entered an arranged marriage. Parvaneh was in her late twenties and had a bit more life experience under her belt. We were both newlyweds and our husbands were cousins.

We both had difficulties in our marriages and perhaps that was the reason we connected. Our secret dates took

45

us away from our families who were telling us how to feel. How to live.

My marriage ended while I was still a teenager. I never saw Parvaneh again. But her heartfelt remarks, that I did not quite understand at the time, were embedded in my heart forever.

I now live in beautiful British Colombia. Many years have passed since those secret meetings, but sometimes I still feel Parvaneh's words. It is as though I somehow got stuck in that stage of my life and never moved ahead emotionally, even though there have been many other changes.

I've been successful at many things since moving to Canada, but my life has always seemed to lack direction. It felt like my identity was stolen from me before I ever had the chance to develop it. This was what Parvaneh had meant on that long-gone rainy day.

I didn't plan my life. Life happened to me. And I did not thrive – only survived.

When the pandemic arrived, I was still working. On my last day of work, something happened with an acquaintance that took me by surprise. It could have jeopardized my career but I decided not to say anything, mostly because the pandemic was changing our lives and we were all trying to understand the new uncertainties. But I felt a sense of disconnection that was not helped by social distancing.

And then I got sick. The doctor diagnosed shingles and told me it was caused by stress. The pressure of the outside world can have an enormous impact on our inner peace. She said shingles usually lasted three to five weeks. I started walking almost every day. With the tranquility, and some natural remedies, I got the shingles under control in a week.

It was also during this time that I started to read a book with a friend. Before the pandemic, we would meet regularly, with the rest of our circle, in the village coffee shop. We could no longer meet in person, so we connected by phone. The book was about inner peace and connecting with our inner child through painting and play. Reading it together gave us comfort.

A few days after we started reading, my friend posted a beautiful painting online.

"I didn't know you could paint," I said.

"I just started," she replied. "It's the book that encouraged me to do it. I connected with an artist who is teaching online to help people during lockdown. You should try it sometime."

"Why would I want to paint something that is already there?" Painting has never really appealed to me. "You might as well take a picture."

"Painting gives me a chance to clear my head for a few hours, without thinking about anything," she replied. "It helps me with my sanity."

Her words floated like brightly-coloured helium balloons in my mind. Painting as a form of meditation. Perhaps I could do that.

I joined her for the next session. Sitting around the table, we followed the instructor's directions: which brushes to use, which colours to choose. Our paintings turned out similar, but each had its own style – a reflection of ourselves.

I created three more paintings and shared them on social media.

Surprisingly, one friend offered to purchase a painting from me. My first custom order!

I needed guidance, so I contacted the instructor who generously walked me through every step of the way and called me an artist.

"I thought I was a student!" I said in surprise.

"You are a new artist," she replied.

Wow! I had found a new way to express myself. I documented my art process every step of the way. Each step was a new level in my personal growth. Something in me shifted, like a small bud of talent that gradually bloomed into a flower. This process helped me realize that I have so many undiscovered buds that deserve my attention. In art, I discovered so many parts of myself, different shades over and over again. What seemed to have withered at age 16, started blooming years later.

The year 2020 has been a hard one, but so much depends on our choices. I chose to die to my old self and grow to the new one. I also learned the importance of connection. The connection between me and my friend gave us the chance to illuminate each other. It reminded me of my dear friend, Parvaneh, who I have not seen in 34 years. In Farsi, her name means butterfly – a symbol for personal transformation. Looking back now, to that day in Tehran, she seems like my guardian angel, with a message for the future – reminding me of who I could someday become.

I recently heard somewhere that painting is not what you do; it is part of who you are. My paintings tell my stories and my stories help to paint my life. My bud has finally found its way to bloom and thrive in so many ways.

WALKING

Jennifer (Lutes) Hill

I have lived in my little green cottage for just a year and it is the first place that has felt like my home. Its yellow door opens onto the sea and each morning I watch the weather drifting across the water. Sometimes my daughters and I fight for space on the chaise in the front window. On other days, the chaise is mine alone. I stay up late, my heart filling with dark sky and darker ocean. More than the house pleasing me, it is my life pleasing me. I'm at the helm of my own boat and I can choose where I go.

Everyone said 2020 would be a wonderful year. I wasn't really in need of new beginnings since I'd carefully constructed a perfectly solo-ish existence. January whistled through like the icy air along the aging edges of my yellow door: fresh and clean but too frigid to be comfortable. This was when I first heard the phrase COVID-19, in connection with a place called Wuhan in Hubei province, China.

Then it was February and by the time the lion ushered in the lamb, my three daughters were making daily Zoom calls and completing school online. My little green cottage was chaos. The combined energy of three almost-grown women and me, escalated kind laughter to dramatic screeching in a matter of seconds. Experience has taught me how to navigate the waves of emotional volatility. I know when to surf it in and when to paddle back to sea. But these tsunamis arrived when I least expected them and diminished at the same astounding speed.

The alternating weeks were worse. After safely delivering the girls to their father, my initial 10 minutes of mental peace quickly gave way to a quiet roaring in my ears where all I could hear was the storm of self-doubt. Divorce is not an easy choice and it's certainly not tidy. The parts I cherish are having the bed to myself and the peace of solitude. The parts I hate are the same. Mothering is not meant to be divided in half.

We have always been a family of walkers. During my first pregnancy we religiously clocked miles on the seawall. On the day our daughter was born, we walked. I slumped on a bench, overdue belly facing the grey water, and burst into tears, patience – and skin – overstretched.

Then it was three, cruising the West Van elevations from beach to nap time. Later, when my husband finished work, we would load the twins in the double stroller and the five of us would cast off. We got to know every inch of that neighborhood: the places where our eldest collected rocks to feed the twins or picked flowers and berries. We walked when we were happy. And sad. We walked early in the morning, roused by crying babies. And on late summer nights we'd bathe the girls then circumnavigate the block in PJs and slippers. We never walked with a destination in mind. We didn't go to get milk or to swing or to teeter-totter. We just walked. Walking became the metronome for our relationship. We tick-tocked back and forth, the five of us tapping out the rhythm of moving in a singular direction.

Lockdown 2020 made sharing the family delicately painful.

Out of the blue, he called: "Do you want to go for a walk?"

I considered. I needed fresh air and adult conversation. So a couple days a week he came for the familiar, but at the same time the new. We walked from my little cottage. The first mile made me bristle, reluctant to be so close to him. All the things I had vanished, were on display: his constant throat clearing, his way of walking too quickly and his headstrong competitiveness which always forced me to walk just a bit further than I wanted.

I insisted that the girls come with us. "Because they need the fresh air," I said, but I meant because I didn't want us to be alone.

We climbed down to the beach at the end of the street only to have to climb back up again to Marine Drive, then up some more. I'd spent 2019 nursing a bad foot and lockdown had been an excuse to do less. By the time I reached the top of the first steps, I was slick with a hot flash. He turned to me and I anticipated the inevitable criticism of my fitness. I was too out of breath to comment when he told the girls to wait for me.

The daughters were uneasy at first and they walked between us, partnering with one or the other, as we do-si-doed this new dance. The route between the beach and the gas station became well-worn. Each time we arrived at the summit the girls lined up to buy some normalcy. We shared bags of artificial cheezies which I had never before allowed, laughing about the orange stains on our faces and our jeans.

Once a week I pled a sore foot and we walked the mostly level route to Dundarave, bumping up against the memories of the previous two decades: family tennis at 29th, walking side-by-side behind the stroller, peering through foliage and cast iron, dreaming about waking to views like that someday. These walks were hard, but they became the figurative structure for the only family this pandemic would allow.

As April showers brought May flowers, the girls acted as if it was 'before.' They ran ahead or stayed behind, all together, and we walked side by side but not too close. We were in synchronicity in our new separateness. I invoked a painful exchange which came from the desire to push hard against a bruise. By increasing the pain temporarily, I hoped it would speed the eventual healing. But the pain stayed put, like the logs that roll up with the high tide and are unmovable in the wet sand. Only when the tide comes back at midnight, can they be carried away, unseen. Pain's salty bittersweetness lodged deep in my throat. I waited for my midnight tide to carry it out to sea.

We continued climbing the hill. And as time passed, I discovered more space for my breath and less bitterness in my mouth. These small journeys have gifted me my children and their father. Five bodies, walking separately, but headed in the same direction.

THE DOUBLE-EDGED SWORD OF 2020

Joanne Singleton

The changes and challenges of 2020 have brought back many treasured memories of West Vancouver in the 1960s.

I remember visiting my grandparents who lived at the end of Mathers Avenue. There were only three homes on the south side of the hilly dead-end street. Over the years, my grandparents lived in two of the homes on Mathers Avenue. The lower one had a beautiful stream running through it with a pool. The one up the hill had a lovely lower garden where my grandmother would sit and feed her friends, the squirrels and the birds.

I have a very clear memory of driving over the Lions Gate Bridge when I was four, on our way to visit Grandma. It was a toll bridge back then.

"Dad, you think there will be houses there one day?" I asked from the backseat, looking at the green mountain range of West Vancouver.

"You just wait honey," he said. "One day, it will be full of houses."

And Dad was right.

Back then, Marine Drive was much quieter than it is now, and we'd always make a stop at Memorial Park. We would walk through the tranquil park to the little bridge where Dad would pretend to be the troll.

"Who's on my bridge?" Dad would growl from below.

My sister, brother and I would run across the bridge screaming and then laughing – again and again. Dad got us every time.

West Vancouver has grown dramatically since those days, both residentially and commercially. But despite the changes, it has retained its unique beauty, and remains a tight-knit community, caring for those who share it.

The emptiness of Dundarave during Phase 1 of COVID-19, reminded me of those early days travelling down Marine Drive, over 55 years ago. At times it was so quiet, you could hear the air swirling as you walked through the streets.

Before the pandemic, Dundarave and Ambleside bustled with activity. People gathered for coffee or lunch, shopped for groceries, or enjoyed the beauty of our spectacular seawall. But with the fear of getting sick, many retreated indoors and a busy community was silenced.

I continued with my walks. I took photographs of the lonely seawall. There were only a few people in the distance, not the usual walkway filled with chatter and smiles. So I watched the ocean, the skies and the wildlife. In silence we blossom. This space created a window of time for reflection, clarity and realization.

When I did cross paths with others, we exchanged a "hello," a smile or a nod of the head. There was an unspoken connection through our eyes, as the face masks covered our smiles. This intentional exchange may not have otherwise happened in the regular course of our busy lives. There was also stepping out of shared airspace or diverting to another path while walking through the crosswalk, down the street or in the stores. COVID-19 has created a multitude of different emotions, reactions and attitudes, as so much was, and still is, unknown.

The stillness of the vacant streets provided me with nature's sounds as accompaniment on my walks. Without the hustle and bustle of passing traffic, I could hear the rapidly flowing creek and birds singing in nearby trees. I became newly-aware and appreciative of my surroundings.

With the extra time on hand, and remaining closer to home, I developed friendships with the crows who visited my yard daily. One brave soul would eat from my hand. He would let me know it was feeding time by swooping down and touching my head or my back. Squirrels, jays, woodpeckers and other birds of varied colours also visited. My grandmother's days on Mathers Avenue seemed to have come full circle.

But the other side of COVID-19 included longer line-ups at the grocery stores. Toilet paper and paper towels were in short supply. Only one purchase per customer was allowed. At times, shelves were bare, labelled out of stock. Masks were required and hands had to be sanitized.

When restrictions were somewhat lifted, it was truly exciting to reunite with the community. Chatting with neighbourhood friends, even masked and at a distance, was like hitting the jackpot. Restaurants and coffee shops were deeply appreciated. Stepping back into Mona's Hair Salon was a complete joy. Not being able to have human interaction, and having your usual routine taken away, makes one much more appreciative of the simple pleasures in life. I now look at life through the lens of gratitude, no matter what comes my way. As my neighbourhood circle has grown, I appreciate new connections more deeply. I've learned more, and I've loved more. Crossing paths, which otherwise might not have been crossed, has made my life fuller.

Most recently though, COVID-19 touched me personally, as someone close to my soul tested positive. Believe me, this is beyond frightening, every moment extremely alarming and concerning. Sleepless nights, racing thoughts, worrying, feeling helpless, not knowing how the virus will take hold. Life can truly change in the blink of an eye, and I am forever grateful and relieved, with a much more settled heart, that recovery has taken place. The effects of COVID linger, but the worst is over.

When we chatted in depth, after the green light was given, she shared her experience: "It's like being in prison. People want to help you, but they really don't know how to. Everyone just hopes you get better. Each day you really hope you'll feel better, but it's like a wave. It's more than the flu. It affects you from head to toe, inside and out. It's scary, it's isolating and it's lonely. Though the experience is downright awful, it does give you time to reflect on what you want in your life; that's when you are not sleeping from extreme fatigue. You then plan to make the changes that you've come to realize, while having this time to reflect. It really makes you question what you want out of *your* life? Just being able to go for a walk is truly amazing!"

As we continue to travel through this extraordinary time in history, I often find myself smiling in response to the displays of caring in this community, like the Dundarave Festival of Lights and Forest of Miracles. West Vancouver is not just a place. It's a "feeling." As we await the arrival of the COVID-19 vaccine, continuing to be safe, let's hope we can soon get back to our daily lives, with more gratitude in our hearts.

FLY ME TO THE MOON

Julie Flynn

Dear Dad,

It's 2 a.m. and I can't sleep. I've been thinking about you a lot lately, especially about the day I arrived at your flat back in September. As I cracked open the door and stepped into the living room, I saw your favourite chair. I imagined you sitting there ready to welcome me. But your chair was empty, and that's when it truly hit me: I would never see you or your smile again.

It has been three months since you passed away, and I still remember your smile like it was yesterday. I wish I could spend one more day with you, visiting one more castle. You did so enjoy visiting the castles. I know the last few years were difficult as your health continued to decline due to diabetes, which you never recovered from in the end.

When you died, it felt like I lost my anchor. I'm feeling so many different emotions: pain, sorrow, anger, disappointment, relief and peace. We last saw each other in February, for your 81st birthday, just before the world went mad. You had just come home from the hospital, and your social worker suggested that you go into a care home, a temporary measure to build up your strength. I knew you didn't want to go, and you blamed me for sending you there. You told me to go back to Canada. I know you didn't mean it, as you always looked forward to my visits. The medication also altered your outlook, and you developed a stubborn streak, which made it difficult for me to help you. You were proud, independent, a true old-fashioned gent, a home bird. You didn't want anyone's help, did you? You wanted to do things your way. I am so sorry that you were never able to leave the care home. You became so very weak.

It's getting close to Christmas here now. I remember the last year I was able to spend Christmas with you in England. That's when I bought you the walker. I knew you didn't like it, and you argued with me for buying it. I selected it in your favourite colour, red, and told you, "It's like having your own Ferrari." I noticed the slight smirk on your face before you told me to throw it in the river; that you would rather fall than use it. You were a feisty old fella, weren't you?

Did you like your funeral? I know you weren't particularly religious, so that's why I thought having a humanist conduct the ceremony was fitting. I liked the focus on your story, your unique qualities, and the relationships you forged. And how about your coffin? I selected the mahogany because the rich reddish-brown was your style. And the deep red roses were also your favourites.

Oh, and what about the songs? You always enjoyed the Rat Pack and Frank Sinatra's album, *Ol' Blue Eyes is Back*. That's why I chose "My Way" for our entry to the crematorium, and "Fly Me to the Moon" as we reflected on your life. And when Al Jolson ended the ceremony with "I'm Sitting on Top of the World," I recalled all the times we used to listen to him when I was a little girl. Do you remember how we would watch old movies and listen to the vinyl records? It's uncanny how I still know the words to most of the songs.

I've been thinking a lot about the day Uncle Davy and I met the humanist at the funeral home, to tell him about your life. Uncle Davy's stories of you as a young lad made me smile. The era when you were a Teddy Boy, which now makes sense as I look at the old photos of you and your mates with those hairstyles. Such impressive hair height, all part of the flamboyant fashion of the times.

I added some of my own treasured memories. Like the time you modified our shoes to become tap shoes, and we mimicked the dance moves of Fred Astaire and Ginger Rogers. I think you secretly harboured a desire to be a dancer.

I also told Uncle Davy about how you taught me to swim at the swimming baths. And how afterwards, we would always have the same sweet treat: a Marathon chocolate bar. It's called Snickers now. I like the original name better, how about you?

After leaving the funeral home, I popped into the supermarket. While I waited in the line-up, I saw a four-pack of Marathon bars between the apples and oranges in the fruit display. I got gooseflesh when I noticed it was a special edition. They hadn't been called Marathon in 30 years. Dad, was this you? It gives me a sense of peace knowing that you are close by.

I bought the bars. I ate one that evening at your flat. Every mouthful brought back memories of those days at the swimming baths.

Thank you for always being there for me. I miss you every day, and I am grateful that you were my dad. I will always be your little girl.

Love,
Julie

THE YEAR ON THE COUCH

Karen Hoffman

I panic-bought six large packs of rice. They splayed on the counter like dead fish. Six is too many. When did I start hoarding? It was early March and my good nature, along with my precious life, were dwindling before my eyes like a short winter day fading into the sunset.

Once a pleasant outing, going to IGA became a worrisome experience. Walking along the village sidewalk was like entering "A Nightmare on Marine Drive." The street was void of people and cars. The sleepy traffic lights blinked yellow. A lone bus rumbled to a stop, stirring up dusty plastic bags. The sound of its brakes ricocheted off the vacant store windows. No one got off the bus. No one got on. The stale grey clouds had the weight of the world on their shoulders. Squawking seagulls dotted the sky.

As the sliding doors of IGA whistled open, time slowed. Shopping list in hand, I entered. Sweet aromas from the bakery fizzled to the ground. Rattling cart wheels overpowered the monotonous store music. The once familiar store seemed transported to another dimension. The air flattened like a forgotten balloon at a six-year-old's birthday party.

Weary shoppers hunched over their carts, snaking up and down the aisles. Beady eyes peered over face masks, darting back and forth, protecting their space. I followed the zombie parade, careful to obey the floor arrows. I had learned my lesson previously when a masked woman scowled at me, saying, "I guess the arrows aren't meant for everyone!" That hurt.

I'm a good person, I screamed in my head. *I'm not the virus!*

White knuckling the cart handle, I joined in the hunt, moving only forward, never back. Forward was the unspoken command. Backwards was punishable by staunch glares. What was happening to my once friendly neighbours? You know, the ones who share in the delight of the beauty and peace of West Vancouver?

The empty shelves were unnerving. Wartime photos flashed through my mind. Drably dressed people lining up for their daily bread. Would that happen here? Could the West Vancouver privileged wear drab clothing? I feared for my neighbourhood.

In the winding cashier lines, carts overflowed. Flour, yeast, chickpeas, tuna and black beans, chips, cookies, popcorn, Lysol cleaning products and hand sanitizer. The coveted toilet paper, in all its importance, sat atop all else like cannons ready for action. Desperate times call for desperate measures. I captured the last six bags of rice.

At home, the rice packs on my disinfected counter waited for instructions. I ran a warm bath in the sink for the fruits and vegetables. If that COVID virus thought it was going to ride in here on a grapefruit, it had another think coming. I manically wiped down each container, then retraced my steps, polishing anything I may have touched or coughed on: counters, doorknobs, light switches, remotes, phones, jewellery, even my face.

Before the apocalypse, in early February, I had returned from a holiday in Palm Springs. Life was ticking along. Work, play, my kids were thriving. My son and his band were finally emerging from my basement and booking gigs in pubs around town. Joy was abundant.

Then that rascal COVID disrupted everything, like a police raid at an all-night strip club. Crafty Corona whirled around the globe leaving wreckage in its wake. Government officials, backed by scientists, asked us to keep six feet apart, wear a mask and wash our hands incessantly. *Above all, do not touch your face!* (It is amazing how much we *do* touch our face.) While most of us followed the recommendations, others defied them.

In generations past, men and women were called to leave home, to go to war. We were called to the couch. Offices, businesses and services closed. Anywhere people could congregate, was shut down: restaurants, schools, gyms and the most difficult, hair salons. The TV prattled on about global disasters: wildfires, hurricanes, oppressive heat, climate change, the ridiculous election in the States, the bizarre outbreak of moths and the insane invasion of murder hornets.

Like a playground bully, COVID demanded everyone's attention. New words and phrases popped up: Zoom, unprecedented, new normal, you have to unmute and – the worst one by far – Karen.

As with any dark cloud, a silver lining emerges. It was a time to go inside. Not just in our homes but ourselves – to self-reflect. It was an opportunity to find out what we were made of, to uncover resources deep within ourselves.

People became adept at gaining weight while nurturing sourdough starter, baking bread and filling fear with homemade muffins. Gardens were planted, and we discovered we could do with less. Even sparks of kindness showed up.

Some things were laughable. Hiking on a trail, people practically dove into the bushes as you passed. Others made exaggerated circles around you like dodging dog droppings. People circumvented each other as if avoiding the plague. Absence of eye contact was awkward, as though you were the uninvited guest at a party. Strolling the salty aired seawall where seals frolicked, seabirds cawed, and freighters honked, you could literally get poked by a six-foot pool noodle for veering too close to another human.

As 2020 comes to a close, my hair looks like my finger got caught in a light socket, my makeup grows stale in the drawer and dressing up means wearing clean elastic-waist pants. I remain grateful. I live in paradise, have my health, humour, family and friends. I can do this.

Oh, and I've stockpiled over 40 different rice recipes.

PERMISSION TO FEEL

Karen Tidball

My West Vancouver home was thick with the stress of unwanted change. The once quiet space had been transformed into a bustling office and school. I was managing my business, working relentlessly on a contentious project. My husband's work filled our basement with intense energy. Our kids brewed in the disruption, irritated by cancelled plans and the loss of their recently-acquired adult freedom. The initial comfort of returning home from school, to escape COVID-19, had worn thin.

I am the anchor for our family. Conversations, searching for answers, arose indiscriminately each day. I stayed still as their waves of emotion rolled towards me, providing them with a sense of solidness so that they did not lose themselves as the tides continued to shift. While I loved being invited into the lives of these humans who are so dear to me, I sometimes struggled to stay balanced, teetering between parent, wife and coach.

By August, six months after the turmoil began, many aspects of life had settled for us. The twins were working and our youngest was preparing to head back to in-person classes at school. My husband had returned to his downtown office, allowing for a much-needed separation between home and work. So I blocked off two weeks of vacation and found myself at the cottage by the lake, a place that has always filled me with joy.

On my first morning there, I felt uneasy when I woke. My eyes struggled to adjust to the sky's glow. I skipped my morning practice of stretches and meditation, opting instead for the kitchen. I warmed my cup with boiling water as I prepared the hot milk and coffee. Then I grabbed a cozy blanket and my iPhone and headed to the outdoor sofa. With the sunlight reflecting off the lake, I settled in. I have always cherished the lull before the day begins.

Sipping my coffee, I scanned the morning news online: how many around the world were affected by the pandemic; how many had died; which country was suffering the most; what were the different strategies of world leaders. The peace I sought was replaced with restless worry. Like a spider, COVID-19 is not always visible. Sometimes it manages to drop into the background, but it still exists in every conversation and action.

My eyes wandered back to the lake and in that moment of appreciating its beauty, the spider leapt. And with it came an onslaught of questions. With so many people suffering in the world, how could I be sitting here, enjoying a vacation? What made me so special that I thought I deserved this luxury?

"I should be doing more," I thought to myself. "I should be helping others, not sitting by the lake. Have I forgotten what it is to struggle?" Tears welled up and a grip tightened around my throat. I put down my phone, reminded myself to breathe and let my emotions echo through my body for the rest of the day.

The following morning I pried open my eyelids, feeling uneasy again. Intuitively, I dragged myself onto the yoga mat, my body remembering how good it feels to rest in corpse pose after crawling out of bed. As I exhaled deeply, emotions hit me like a rogue wave. I responded by releasing my muscles and melting into the ground, knowing it would support me.

And then I gathered myself up and began to journal.

My words flowed onto paper, as my body sighed deeply. My shoulders rose in acknowledgment of my reality. It had been emotionally exhausting supporting our kids, my husband and managing my work. There had been the pressure of online exams, the lack of summer work, the uncertainty around school return, and the loss of outside commitments. And the conversations with my husband had been unusually tense as we navigated conflicting views on how to live and work under these curious circumstances. I had also been trying to ensure that my in-laws felt supported. And wondering if the social distancing from my brother and sister-in-law was good enough. The voice in my head dictated as I wrote, my thoughts coloured by COVID-19. The emotional energy was overwhelming. *Of course* I was tired.

Now, months later, I can smile at that moment. With all that I have learned over the years, I am sometimes still blind to old habits: discrediting my own emotions, doing too much or thinking that I should be doing more. Taking care of the people who matter most to me is always my first priority. To do this well, I know that I must also take care of myself. But on occasion, when life takes an unexpected turn, the habit of falling victim to the I-should-do-more voice returns. It's so familiar, that I often don't see it until I give myself time to reflect, name and accept. Once it's finally revealed, though, the awareness refills my spirit and helps me stay grounded in the midst of ongoing shifts. Like the pandemic.

My son recently said, "Mom, I have come to realize that routine is highly underrated."

The wisdom of his words connected deeply with what I know to be true. With that in mind, the gift I add to my daily routine is a new practice, one I rarely miss, not even for coffee. Each day I meditate, stretch and reflect on what I am grateful for. I also reflect on the things I have recently done that make me proud. And I finish with a declaration for this new day I am blessed to have in front of me. Being kind to myself and being in gratitude shapes my days, filling me with hope, appreciation and energy. It restores me.

I am ready for whatever comes next.

WEIGHT

Kimberley Clarke

I usually don't ruminate on the glum. I try to sally forth, stiff upper lip-ly, but this year has been a doozy. I am not yet wobbling, not screaming uncle, but there have been moments when I would have loved to succumb. But here's the thing. I can't. I just can't. Too many people depend on me. To be me. Goofy. Competent. In control. But how does one control chaos? With a smile dammit and memories of better, simpler days. Like January 2020.

The year, in all its glorious ignorance, started with such promise. But then…

February hit and my husband's brother, renowned microbiologist Dr. Frank Plummer – Order of Canada recipient, Aids researcher extraordinaire, SARS saviour, EBOLA conquerer, Theresa Tam's mentor, Anthony Fauci's pal – died. I swear, he could have saved us all from this COVID mania. He died in the place that he loved –

Nairobi, Kenya. He died during the fortieth anniversary celebrations of the Universities of Manitoba and Oxford Aids project. A heart attack at lunch.

My husband and I flew to Winnipeg for his memorial. It was the weekend that the news about COVID broke. A terrible irony really. If only Frank's heart knew how much the world needed his brilliance right at that moment. And now. If only.

Two weeks later, the world was in lockdown. Schools closed indefinitely. Highways were lonely. Our family, like everyone, was trying to make the best of it. We became instant hoarders, fanatic cleaners, mad online shoppers.

My husband's eyes turned a mild curry yellow. Rarely a good colour, unless it is in a kitchen. His liver, it seemed, had had enough. Decided that it would like to live elsewhere. Good timing I guess. No one was working. Neither was his liver.

I continued to teach.

Online meetings with colleagues, homework assignments with students via email. Accessible 24/7. No need to sleep. There was always coffee.

And then the dog. Of course. The dog – my husband's constant companion, his magical muse, his stinky little buddy – needed to be put down.

I would need to find a replacement. For the dog.

What saved my husband was the news. Political theatre. Oh, and a new recliner, for lying about. Why get up when the wind can blow you over? No muscle, just sinew. From big and robust to twig-like in four short months.

We used to joke about friends who wallowed in their achey joints. But here we were, measuring our days with pills and drainage and elastic waist monkey pants. Monkey pants because the pockets weren't deep enough. Things flew out of them when he sat, when he stood. With their balloon-y shaped legs, they made him feel like an organ grinder's dancing pet.

I continued to teach.

Back in the building we went.

Stop, sanitize, separate.

September. October. November. December.

Fearful of bringing home the virus, I would change my clothes in the garage and shower before going upstairs to the "medical wing."

"I can't get sick," I'd whisper, slathering antibacterial goop all over myself, donning an array of masks. "Who would be me?"

The children were worried. They worked in service industries. They stayed on their side of the bridge. The one in the basement stayed there. He too was frightened. But it might have been of us.

I continued to teach.

During my daily commute, in my forty-five minute sing-along escape bubble, I thought. About being a kid and not believing that kids become responsible adults. I planned to always be a kid and wildly akimbo. I thought about how protected I was. How I loved Barbies and my imagination. How I would make up stories for hours. How I wrote poetry, and tried to compose music on our old upright piano. How I would dream in French, or so I thought. How I spent so much time alone and was never happier than when I was listening to records, dancing "the pony" like a maniac on my red shag rug in my black and white room. This "free" time, this driving, this living in my head, this nostalgia, allowed me to find the happy. So I sang my anthem, "Build me up Buttercup," at the top of my lungs.

But I am no fool.

I will continue to teach and pay attention to the road ahead because I know that all these memories are lies. Lies of my own making that make it easier to live than in the here and now, because waiting for change tests one's patience, one's upper lip. But there is a smidge of comfort knowing that the sun always rises and that change is constant. Even if you can't get a liver at the speed of light from Amazon, you know it will materialize when you least expect it. So you keep your bag packed at the front door while you wait for the call. You browse puppy photos and know that the perfect little buddy will find you and that ultimately patience – doggedness – will pay out. And that's probably why I keep looking at real estate listings. Not because I want to move, really, but because I want to feel the comfort of my childhood home, where it is always summer, where my stories are just unfolding, and where someone – everyone – looks after me. But until then I'll continue to teach, and sing really loudly and out of tune, about buttercups.

LIGHT UP YOUR FACE WITH GLADNESS

Lindy Hughes Pfeil

My favourite birthday present – ever – was the bright red record player my father gave me when I turned thirteen. Because pocket money was not a thing in our household, and I was not old enough to have a job, I had to wait for Christmases and more birthdays for my own records. In the meantime, I listened to my father's collection. Joni James. Frank Sinatra. Louis Armstrong. Nat King Cole.

I spent hours singing to my reflection in the bedroom window, committing every song to memory. "Blue Moon." "The Lord's Prayer." "A Kiss to Build a Dream On." From Joni I learned that if I walked with hope in my heart, even in the darkest of storms, I would never walk alone. Louis convinced me that it really is a wonderful world. And Frank urged me to do it my way.

But it was Nat King Cole I loved. His voice was a hot water bottle on a winter's night. And the song that lodged itself in my bones was "Smile." Even though your heart is breaking, Nat sang, "You'll find that life is still worthwhile. If you just smile." I hung onto those words with every ounce of teenage angst. And, for the next four and a half decades, I did exactly that: smiled. Through the moves – so many of them – changing homes, schools, jobs, I smiled. Through travel, marriage, births, deaths, immigration, I smiled. Through joy and loss, love and disappointment. Uncertainty. I smiled.

And then, in slunk 2020.

I was working at an elementary school when, in an effort to curb the spread of COVID-19, learning went online. I met the students in little pockets of virtual reality, my role loosely defined as "social-emotional support." School work was not so much the problem. Connection was the issue. Isolated children. Anxious parents. The unknown.

Sometimes we played games. I asked questions. Who did they most admire in the world? What superpower would they choose? What did they have for breakfast? We drew pictures together – apart – of places we wanted to visit when the pandemic was over, of rainbows, sparkly unicorns, monsters, darkness. They showed me their precious treasures. And the realities of their lives.

In a peculiar way, the little screen between us encouraged greater honesty. Vulnerability. There were tears. Outbursts. Silences. Connections.

One morning I asked the children to bring their baby photos to our meeting. I brought one of three-year-old me and my father. On a trampoline. A *real* trampoline, not one of those contraptions that hover precariously above the ground on wonky legs. This one was constructed over an enormous hole in the ground, secured in place by heavy metal springs.

In the photo, my father is crouched on the outside edge, his arm reaching across the springs, holding my hand. His elbow is angled just so, to help me jump higher. The tension in his wrist, the way he leans towards me, every muscle and tendon in his body, speaks love. A frown of concentration – and concern – wrinkles my forehead, and all ten of my fingers clutch at his hand. But I am smiling. Despite the fear. Because he is holding onto me. And the thing I know, even as a toddler, without having the words for it, is that my father would die to protect me.

June came. I said goodbye to my students and their families. I taped the photo of me and my father to the mirror above my chest of drawers.

The pandemic continued. My own family started unraveling in a way I never imagined possible. I have always been an iffy wife, but now my parenting skills were proving abysmal too.

I did the only thing I could think to do: I laced up my purple hiking shoes and walked out the door. No destination in mind. And as my feet stomped across this land I call home, I thought about how we had got here. I reflected on the choices, the turning points, the vows made so long ago. For worse. In sickness. Sometimes death is not the ugliest kind of parting there is. A broken heart, I discovered, is not a metaphor.

I was thankful for Dr. Bonnie's mandated masks. I was all out of smiles.

And then, quite by chance, I discovered my father's secrets.

A cousin I had known only briefly in childhood, reconnected with me in cyberspace. She told me stories about my father I had never before heard: the reason that he and his nine siblings were raised in orphanages and foster care. Stories of loss. Betrayal. And violence.

I looked at the photo taped to my mirror, my father so fiercely gentle. How had he survived being hurt so deeply by those he most trusted? I wish I could have asked him how he had turned that hurt into such spectacular love for me and my sister. Perhaps his advice would have made me a better parent. But he died long before I became a mother. As the world continued spinning, I continued walking. In the sun. In the wind. The rain. Now though, I listened to music. Music I had not heard in decades, but had never forgotten. My father's music. And I cried, my teenage angst now multiplied by midlife and a virus that was showing no respect for boundaries. I cried for my students. For my own children. For my father's lost childhood.

I would never again, I said to myself, smile.

One miserable morning, as I walked beside the Salish Sea, I wondered if, perhaps, it was *music* that saved my father. He could neither keep time, nor a tune. But this did not stop him from playing the banjo, the guitar and the mouth organ. Or from singing – loudly – the songs from his record collection.

"I want to be in that number!" he would belt out, eyes glinting yellow-black. "Oh when the saints go marching in!"

Perhaps it was there, in the lyrics of those musical giants, that Pa discovered possibility. Healing. How to be a father, despite the terrible things that had happened.

So, as my purple shoes sidestepped the puddles on Marine Drive, I listened closely, trying to hear what my father might have heard. What *I* had heard as a 13-year-old, singing along with my little red record player.

Louis Armstrong sang about skies of blue and I noticed the white dragons floating above my head. Joni James whispered that I should walk with my head held high and I saw the dandelions, inexplicably sprouting on the rockface. When it was Frank Sinatra's turn, I found the heart-shaped pebble of pitch on the side of the road.

And then, just as my shoes headed home, it was Nat King Cole, singing about fear and sorrow. About uncertainty. I spotted one pink bud on the raggedy rosebush in our driveway. Stubbornly resisting winter, it was blooming – despite the pandemic, the world's incquities and my inability to fix my family.

"Light up your face with gladness," Nat crooned through the wind and injustice. "Hide every trace of sadness."

I leaned into the rosebush, dodging thorns.

"You'll find that life is still worthwhile."

My icy fingers cupped the hardy little blossom. It was not just alive. With its brash pinkness, it was laughing in the face of 2020.

I smiled.

AN OASIS

L. Noël

Pulling back the rug.
Picking at a scab.
Tearing off that strip of wax – exposing that underlying
prickling of red.

It feels like we always knew, yet chose to live in the
shadows.
How do we manoeuver the chaos?
Impossible.

Just handle what you can – whatever that is.
I preach this, yet I seldom practise it.

I want to reimagine so much.
From my little mountain of what I am grateful for –
constantly grasping at the slipping pieces of sand –
slithering between my fingertips.

Everything that could be.
Can this world truly evolve without repeating past harms?
I want more.

Me, wanting more?

Just like Ariel,
I wanna be where the people are. I wanna see, wanna see
them dancing.

But that's not all. Not even close.

People tell me that they are learning to cope with less and
are also losing their patience.
People tell me about loves that used to be. They tell me
about the echoes and the hurt and how some strive to
make life better for the little humans they made, while
others seem to try their best to hurt, harm and injure those
that we are trying to fix things for.
The band-aid kind. The one we don't like to talk about.
Is that all we have left?

But what do I know? I have my little moments but I don't
have to worry about a little person. Do I want to?
I don't know.
Who knows.
Hurt can change so much.

We know this.

But how do we make those who like to hurt know this?

Hurt people, hurt people – we know this too.

I have an oasis. It is where my mother and my father live. They made a garden – oozing with flowers, fruit and vegetables. Hummingbirds dart towards honeysuckles draped on trellises. Dogwood flowers sparkle from between deep green cedars and squash tumbles down the rock face. Cheeky white strawberries peek out from under their leaves as beets and carrots burrow and surface simultaneously next to the mural of peas and beans. Leeks thicken slowly while blueberries blanket their bushes, awaiting our arrival donning milk jug buckets that are ready to be dotted with fruit.

Perfect for an apocalypse. I go there when I want to admire what the earth can do and the fruitful efforts of those I come from.

I go there to be, for some moments.

I wonder if they thought, nearly thirty years ago, you will have a daughter – oh, here she is, crying – born on a full moon, much like tonight.

This daughter – she will seek snippets of solace with you in a moment in time where those you love are untouchable.

She will be just fine. You knew she would be, but you will have taught her that home is where we are together – comfort in that rocktop oasis.

Don't worry mom, she will make good choices that year. She will move into a place that is good. She will get a job that makes her happy and is interesting. She has phenomenal friends and a great relationship with that other daughter you will have soon.

Yet another accident. Apparently.

That other daughter has a fluffy baby of her own. He is perfect. The Zac Efron of puppies according to Chel. He gets kidnapped by his aunt twice a week. He is one of her little lights during that time.

Oh yes, 2020. And that daughter who comes over to be in the garden?
She will make mistakes that year – but the kind you learn from. She will be taken care of and appreciated, but she will relish how she can get in her little tiny car and come to you.

As we exist on this unceded land. As we create moments in a way we never thought we would have to. As our actions impact people more than ever before – there can be love and there can be home.

Sometimes those are much closer to the surface than we realize and perhaps, without touch, we have to rely on other ways of revealing what lies underneath. The underbellies of our souls that manage to avoid the light for most of our lives. The vulnerable, ghastly parts of us that come out when it is not easy, when we are not ok. The me that has to desperately cling on to what she needs in moments where it is unclear but there must be something.

Who is that me?
Who is that you?
Can we help each other?

Maybe.

Living in a world that feels smaller every day and vaster every second. I call it Paradox City.

As I fall deeper into acknowledging the parts of me that have reared their heads in this land of opposites – the parts that differ in their opinions – it can make us stand stronger upon our ground.
Less wobbly, perhaps.

Maybe our morals can become less chaotic as we try to find and gain control.

How much of human behaviour is an attempt to find just that?
Some semblance of control?

I like chaos. At least I think I do. I don't want to know what is going to happen next. At least I thought I didn't. Until what happened next was no longer hugging those I love.

It turns out predictability of my ability to express love was something I liked controlling.

Control and change – they might be distant ex-lovers or alienated cousins.
What is it they say? The only thing that is eternal is this very moment, as your eyes peruse this page, your brain miraculously taking in lines and squiggles to internalize them into your very own interpretation of the words I am currently typing. Yes... this exact moment.

That tingly feeling. You know the one?

The one you feel when someone does something for you that they shouldn't have – the kind of "shouldn't have" that is dripping with love and care and you can't compute why someone would have taken the time to do it.

Perhaps it is the free Sprite your server gave you at the restaurant. That smile from a stranger that got you through the most horrendous of days. Or maybe the words someone said that were especially for you and truly managed to touch your soul.

The way I feel, especially now. What I can share, what I will never be able to, and everything in between. My sneaky mind and its particular way of seeing this earth and its beings. I feel. Unabashedly. I like how I feel, even though it can hurt.

The love it boils and bubbles and at times it wants to burst free – shattering me.

It is a privilege to shatter.

CONSTRUCTING
A TROPHY WIFE

Melody Noble

I am a Trophy Wife.

I never dreamed of being a West Vancouver Trophy Wife, but I am 18 years my husband's junior, and I have the traditional pale skin, blond hair, and blue-eyed beauty of the girl next door. And, despite not applying for the job, my husband has given me the financial comfort to be at home, not working.

This contrasts starkly with my previous life, where I woke up bleary-eyed at 5 a.m., dressed my daughter for daycare, and sucked down a quad shot espresso. This fueled my day of running room to room, giving pain injections, holding trembling hands, and comforting post-surgical patients in their confused, drugged state. I was a surgical nurse at North Hawaii Community Hospital, working the "crap shifts" – twelve-hour night-shifts, weekends and holidays. I lived paycheck to paycheck, helping my daughter with her homework and planning occasional beach days.

My dream job was the weekday, day-shift rotation at the hospital. I also coveted the part-time nursing position at the local private school, which would give me discounted tuition for my daughter.

John changed everything.

He was my neighbour, who waved when we drove by. When I hosted the rowdy neighbourhood game night, he brought over fancy snacks and wine. The rest of the neighbours brought stale chips and drank my beer. He was super gregarious, telling stories and amusing my daughter with annoyingly corny dad jokes.

"How can you tell when a joke is a dad joke?" John asked. "It's a-parent." We became friends.

John is a Canadian goose, migrating to Hawaii during the rainy Canadian winter and returning home to West Vancouver when the ski trails have transformed into hiking routes. In Canada, he is a big-time barrister. In Hawaii, he is a farmer, managing a permaculture macadamia nut farm, donating the yield to the community. He expertly designed and built an off-the-grid, open-air house which overlooks the ocean and his farm.

He is the opposite of me – the girl who grew up with an outhouse and traveled only by reading books about foreign places.

John provided me with a happy distraction, by taking me to the hometown rodeo, where we watched children compete, clinging to the fleece of sheep, which was more entertaining than their dads riding the bucking bulls. We swam with the giant turtles at the quiet locals' beach. We went to the local Jazz night, ate fresh Hawaiian sushi and drank cocktails made with orange, passionfruit and guava.

As we explored our little town of Honokaa, we got to know each other. We had great conversations, and discovered that, surprisingly, we had a lot in common. Both of us are fiercely independent, love travel, enjoy reading a book more than watching a movie, value education, and oddly enough, we both played rugby at university.

One sunset evening, lounging on a beach blanket at Puako beach, we were watching the tiny crabs dance away from the crashing waves. John surprised me by ducking in for a kiss. It was warm and natural, not awkward or demanding. Our relationship mirrored that kiss, and continued to progress naturally.

I hadn't realised until then, that he was dating me. I would never have dated him. I cringed at the thought of being lost in another messy relationship. However, it was too late. I already had feelings for him and his offers to explore the hidden beaches were irresistible.

We started traveling together. Impulsively, I hopped on a plane to Vancouver. We spent the summer on *Baloo*, his cozy, 36-foot C&C sailboat, sailing through the breathtaking Desolation Sound.

The icy air, untouched landscape and serene isolation in Canada reminded me of my childhood, growing up in the Last Frontier, Alaska. Desolation Sound's windy bite, the haggard trees that somehow survive along the rocky cliffs, the shouting waves along the coastline, and the fellowship of the silent whales and barking seals alongside our boat brought a new, but familiar feeling. I found my new home.

After that summer, John didn't have to work hard at wooing me to move to West Vancouver. I fell in love with British Columbia, as much as with him. I uprooted my life and moved into his. While we were reading on the couch, in the same way he would have offered me coffee, he casually asked me to marry him.

I opened my mouth to say, "You're ridiculous." Instead, I said "Yes."

We had both been married previously, so we knew negotiations and trade-offs were required. We honestly discussed finances, our flaws, our families, the chores, medical issues and what we wanted in a marriage. He wanted a wife at home to greet him at the door with a dry martini and a kiss when he returned from work. He despised dishwashing machines. I wanted stability and my financial worries to disappear. I also wanted a bidet and Taco Tuesdays.

"Kids?" I asked. We already had my animated, adventurous daughter, who would be leaving the house in a few years. Did he want to start again? And did he realize the implication of this question? I was a whisper away from forty and we would need to begin any baby-making process immediately.

"Definitely," he said enthusiastically. "We will have two more children." Perhaps his confidence came from being accustomed to getting what he wants, or that he was only responsible for five minutes of a nine-month baby-making project.

And so our family adventure began, and quickly. We sailed over to Gibsons and got married on the Salish Sea. Marrying him, I won more than the lottery. John is dashingly handsome, witty, always pairs the correct cheeses, and cooks us rich, French-inspired dinners.

Within two months of being an "official" West Vancouver Trophy Wife, I was pregnant with our happy, musical boy, Donald.

As I look out my kitchen window, while sipping my Salt Spring Island coffee, sweetened with our farm's light macadamia nut honey, I contemplate my journey from nurse to wife. Seeing the choppy whitecaps, I am enticed to go sailing, knowing that the calm sea is coming this afternoon. I am so grateful for the sea, for my home, for being able to enjoy the day, even for my sweet coffee.

My quiet reflection is interrupted by the faint whimpering of baby Odin needing a fresh diaper. Soon, Donald's sticky hands will be handing me a juice cup to refill before our morning walk through the trails of Whytecliff Park. I savour mothering my children, immersing myself in nature, and following my passion for writing. I still have the "crap shift" – long nights, weekends and holidays – and now making my husband's martini. In spite of this, my posh, supposedly superficial career is the most fulfilling and rewarding one I can imagine. I appreciate being a West Vancouver Trophy Wife.

NEW BEGINNINGS PROVOKED BY THE STENCH OF SMOKE

Rose Lepin

On February 8, 2020, my world turned upside down.

It was a regular Saturday night on Kings Avenue. I had just finished a voice recital and we arrived home to our Dundarave garden suite, Blizzards in hand. The chilly air struck my bare legs as I entered the house, and I decided to take a bath.

Later, as I was getting out of the tub, the light above me dimmed for a moment, then brightened. Assuming it was an issue with the bulb, I simply turned it off. I spent the next hour in bed, in my towel, scrolling mindlessly through TikTok, as 15-year-olds do on Saturday evenings.

As I reached for my pyjamas, my fraternal twin sister, Gracie, hustled into my room. She said she smelled smoke and had heard panicked footsteps upstairs. Before she could finish her sentence, our mother, Susan, came crashing through the front door.

"Girls! Get out of the house!" It was the kind of scream I had never heard before.

No time, no preparedness ... no clothes. As Gracie ran, I threw on a long summer dress and fleece bathrobe. Bolting out the door in my hand-me-down Uggs, I didn't even feel the cold.

The black smoke billowing from the roof was like something from a cartoon, near-opaque. Mom was trying to get our landlords out from their suite, exposing herself to smoke inhalation.

As she screamed at them, I screamed at her: "Mom! Don't be like *This is Us!*"

She got out quickly. Our elderly landlords took a few more moments to emerge. The police got to the scene first. They documented the surroundings and asked if we needed anything. The time it took the firemen to get there, felt simultaneously like seconds and years. As soon as they arrived, they pulled out the hoses.

Mom, Gracie and I stood across the street, motionless, watching as flames pierced the roof, creating an uncontrollable wave of fire. I didn't cry. Instead, I laughed. It was all I had in me.

We called my father, who was visiting Kelowna, to tell him what had happened, and we updated our friends via social media. We warmed up under the dim, incubator-esque red lights of the fire truck.

Eventually, one of the police officers drove us to a family friend in Caulfeild. We entered timidly through their mud room, unsure of what to say. I think they felt the same. This was new terrain for everyone. Gracie and I both gave a variation of "Thanks for letting us stay here," and shuffled to the kitchen. We told them everything we knew, which was virtually nothing. What could possibly have started a fire that huge in such little time?

We had the option of staying at our father's presently-unoccupied house in Horseshoe Bay, but the three of us agreed that we needed to be around people. Our mother's friend shuttled us down to Dad's house to retrieve whatever belongings we could find. When we got there, I realised how many belongings I carry back and forth between parents each week – I couldn't even find underwear at Dad's, let alone pyjamas. I grabbed what I could.

Later that night, we got a call from the fire department. The spark had ignited in the attic. Since we lived in the lower half of the house, we didn't even know an attic existed. The origin was electrical, it seemed, and there was nothing we could have done.

Mom, Gracie and I exchanged glances, recalling that we had each seen the lights dim and brighten. But each of us had thought it was an isolated occurrence in our respective rooms. None of us could remember a smoke alarm going off on either level of the home. We tried not to think about what could have happened if the fire had started an hour or two later, once we were already asleep. We felt grateful for our lives.

While the days following were intense with grief and chaos, the overwhelming feeling, for me at least, was gratitude for the people who came together to help us. I felt humbled by the support from friends and family, not only across the country, but all over the world. We had only lived in that happy little suite for nine months, but boy did we love it.

After the premises had been double, triple, quadruple checked for hotspots or any other threats, we were permitted to enter with smoke-proof masks to retrieve whatever belongings had survived. Our floor was damaged by smoke, water and chemicals, but no flames had touched it. My feet sloshed through the soggy carpets, and it felt like the set of a post-apocalyptic movie.

Not even a week before, we were going about our daily activities, counting on having our little suite to return to. With a single spark, the trajectory of our lives spun out of control. We walked through the mess left behind. Luckily, most belongings stored in drawers, boxes and cupboards survived. This meant I could recover my computer, which was in a closed backpack.

The bag I was most worried about, was my makeup bag. It may sound shallow but makeup has never failed to bring me serenity, even in the hardest of times. I love the collection I have gathered over the past few years. But my products and tools would only be safe to use if my bag was closed at the time of the fire. Much to my relief, it was. Not only did I recover my old makeup, but a neighbour gifted Gracie and me numerous like-new products that she wasn't using anymore. We didn't know this neighbour personally; she heard about our situation through the grapevine. This is just one example of the kindness and generosity we experienced in the aftermath of that cursed Saturday.

I am a very different person now than I was on that morning in February. I have new views on the world, and new anxieties. All those ingredients make up who I am. Losing my home this year was one of *many* steppingstones.

THE PHOENIX RISES OUT OF ADVERSITY

Sharon Selby

She calls me her phone, but almost never uses me for phone calls. Her hands claw around me, as she stares at me for hours: Instagram stories, Snapchat snaps, TikTok videos, news feeds, YouTube, and incoming messages. Day and night, she scrolls and scrolls.

My owner's name is Alex, and this is 2020.

Images of koala bear and kangaroo rescues, bushfires and burned homes, pain me as they fill my screen. A Ukrainian plane has been shot down. There is so much tragedy to absorb, and Alex is questioning whether World War III is a possibility. She types non-stop, unaware of her increasing internal angst. As she texts, the tension between the US and Iran is mounting.

"What if this is the beginning of World War III?" she and her friends ask each other.

On the same day, there is a flood of pictures and comments about Prince Harry and Meghan Markle. What is happening? The Duke and Duchess of Sussex announce, on Instagram of all places, that they're stepping down from the Royal Family. It is unheard of to make such an announcement on phones like me, instead of traditional newspapers or the BBC news. Over 1.8 million Instagram "likes" and the British monarchy is shaken.

More tragedy follows: Los Angeles Laker basketball legend, Kobe Bryant, his 13-year-old daughter, Gianna, and seven others have died in a helicopter crash. Alex stares at me in disbelief. Can this really be true? Heartfelt messages are pouring out on my screen. She holds me in shock, tears streaming. She is a big fan of Kobe Bryant, and his daughter was just one year younger than her. Now she's dead, in an instant. The year 2020 is off to a tumultuous start.

The World Health Organization announces that a deadly coronavirus, COVID-19, has emerged in Wuhan, China, and is spreading across the globe. I feel Alex's pulse rapidly beating. She watches people in China screaming in pain, falling to the ground. Her anxiety is high, and it's transmitting through her clammy hands, to me. I can hardly keep up with the bombardment of postings.

Stop, Alex! Please! I want to shout. *Don't you see how this is affecting you? You're a sensitive soul, and these images stay in your mind for weeks after you've watched them.*

But I can't stop her. She's glued to the heart-wrenching Instagram videos. Post after post shows patients on ventilators fighting for their lives. Nurses and doctors speak through me, recording panicked messages about the shortage of beds, staff and supplies.

Fear is contagious. I am deeply concerned about Alex's mental health. She's not getting enough sleep since she can't switch me off at night. She is seeing too much and there are no filters. Raw images and videos come at her, and she's sucked in. She can't stop checking. The virus is spreading. The numbers are mounting. Her anxiety is escalating.

Oh Alex, if only you would turn me off and give yourself a break from it all.

On March 11, the World Health Organization declares a global pandemic. The disease is spreading, and everything is shutting down. Restaurants, shops, gyms, tennis courts, playgrounds and schools – even Disneyland – have closed until further notice. The Olympics are postponed, Spring Break trips cancelled, and education is going online. Her classroom will be a Zoom room.

I despair for Alex at the thought of even more time spent on screens, but Zoom is the new word. She uses it as a verb, "I'll Zoom you," as a noun, "Let's meet on Zoom," and as an adjective, "Let's have a Zoom party." New hashtags pop up as new lingo emerges. #LockDownNow #SocialDistancing #StayHomeStaySafe #FlattenTheCurve #MaskUp #MyPandemicSurvivalPlan #Coronapocalypse #PanicBuying and more.

Images of deserted roads, empty shelves and the last rolls of toilet paper go viral. Hand sanitizer is sold out and masks are a hot commodity. Toilet paper memes trend and people offer pizzas in exchange for loo rolls! Two women in an empty toilet paper aisle play the *Titanic* theme song on their violins. This meme makes Alex laugh. It's a relief to hear her giggle.

On May 25, African American, George Floyd, is choked to death by police. Alex is fuming! She watches the recording over and over. She gasps each time she hears George Floyd saying, "I can't breathe." Her eyes fill.

#BlackLivesMatter is everywhere and racial tension explodes. All over the world, people take to the streets in support of the Black Lives Matter movement.

On June 5, I attend the Vancouver anti-racism rally with Alex. It's really loud, but peaceful. Thousands are here in support, chanting. It's the midst of COVID and I can just see into Alex's eyes behind her mask. She looks sad and exhausted. The world seems so out of control and unpredictable right now. So much suffering. Alex is feeling the intensity of the emotions surrounding her.

On August 4, I ring. It's Alex's cousin, Aleyna, calling from Beirut, Lebanon.

"There's been an explosion," she sobs. "Chemicals stored at the Beirut port exploded, and everything is gone. We've been ripped to shreds. So many people have died, and thousands are wounded. Our homes are gone."

"How can this be?" Alex asks. "Are you all okay?"

Her heart hurts, thinking of her aunts, uncles and cousins. Her hands shake and her body trembles. She hands me to her mom, to continue the conversation.

"It's so unfair," she cries, for her relatives and for beautiful Beirut. "What is happening to our world?"

Alex, it's been a very tough year. Your angst and anxiety is understandable, but you will get to the other side of this. There has been a lot of loss, but you are building resilience. You have had no choice but to learn to adapt. You have learned the importance of staying in the present and appreciating what you do have. Joining in with your neighbours to bang pots and pans at 7 p.m., night after night, and creating hearts for the front window to applaud the front-line workers, are memories you will always cherish. This extra time with your family has brought you all closer. You truly understand Dr. Henry's words, "Be Kind. Be Calm. Be Safe." This has been a year like no other, but just as the phoenix rises out of adversity, you will emerge stronger as well, dear Alex.

A COVID-19 JOURNAL

Sharon Thompson

There is a photo on my screensaver of me in Thailand on the first day of 2020. In a field of midnight darkness I crouch close to the earth, hands stretching up to the New Year sky, releasing a flaming paper lantern into a universe of intentions. It's on my phone, to remind me of all I need to let go, to open up space for new inspirations. Mounting change and responsibility in recent years have created a cluttered sense of purpose. 2020 was to be a reset. COVID-19 was not the reset I had in mind.

December 25, 2020: Reflections
During a family hike through Lighthouse Park, I reflect to my daughter: "This time last year I was on my way to meet you in Thailand." This statement, and all that has happened since, triggers an avalanche of memories that renders me silent for the rest of our Christmas Day hike. As my feet curl around roots and rocks, I thumb a delicate new ring which draws a sweet sting to my eyes and tugs at my heart.

It's an "Isla" ring – a Christmas gift from my daughters. We emerge onto a magnificent stony outcrop against the crashing sea. Can anyone step into this space and not be taken with the awe of it all? In the chaos of the past year, a simple moment like this, grounds me to the here and now and as the ocean air swirls around me, I reflect on all the ways we have adapted to change and how curiosity has morphed into inspiration.

March 2020: When things really change
Walking through my front door after being instructed to work from home is surreal. Within the wonderment, is a glimmer of calm that brings unanticipated balance and contentment. Letting go of commuting times and holding virtual meetings creates more space in my day. Chores are accomplished around meetings and my days open up for more recreational activity. The spring weather is beautiful so I contemplate my first vegetable garden.

April 2020: The love of something new
Is there anything more charming than a kitten's curiosity? My biggest joy this year is my winter kitten, Isla. A surprisingly clumsy kitten with saucer wide eyes and possum-like body, she is a fur-ball of love, more like a regal dog than a frisky kitten. She is full of curious quirks but none more adorable than when she places her paw in the palm of my hand as we drift off to sleep together.

May 2020: Inspirations
I laugh at myself now, so proud of my grand idea to grow vegetables. Clever Sharon! What a smart thing to do – reducing unnecessary outings. My pride and I set off to purchase seeds and sowing materials. Instead of matching my enthusiasm the garden clerk rewards me with an eye-rolling remark, "COVID has made *everyone* a farmer."

Regardless, it is entirely satisfying to plant row upon row with mounds and clusters here and there, imagining how it will sprout, bloom and harvest. As I garden, I marvel at Isla chasing butterflies, growing more agile as she discovers all the wonders of the outdoors.

July 2020: The new normal?
The pace and uncertainty of work hasn't altered but within the COVID storm is my home sanctuary. It's a peaceful place where I can come to terms with all the concerns and hardships swirling around our community. I step into my garden office daily, plugging into meetings with coffee and garden hose in hand. The family gathers every Wednesday for takeout to support our local businesses and I send them home with my daily harvests. It's the most habitual gathering we've had since they left home and it feels good.

August 2020: Isla
It's mid-afternoon and I'm working on my deck. Isla is camouflaged in a nearby patch of wheat-coloured grass, stalking insects. As I tap away at my computer I feel a gust of air at my back. Turning, I see two coyotes breeze past me. Within seconds, they scoop up Isla and disappear. Horrified, I jump in my car to follow and catch up to them in a nearby cul de sac. Isla is draped in one coyote's jaws. I chase them shrieking, clapping, stomping. The coyote drops Isla. Thank goodness. I pick up her limp body, holding her tenderly, hoping that my warmth will revive her. But she is gone. Cradling her closely, I drive home to my daughter. We both melt to the ground in disbelief. Eventually we clean her up, curl her into a peaceful ball and place her in a crafted box. The next day I find myself alone, speechless and numb, not knowing how to honour Isla. An angel of a friend, blessed with a gift for honouring life, arrives to help me. Together, we find a place to lay Isla to

rest. We sprinkle flowers and soil from the garden and share meaningful words. We build security, plant a white hydrangea over her, and sit quietly together. It is perfect. I feel immense gratitude and let go of two things that day.

November 2020: COVID sets up camp
Fall is a settling period. Masks and distancing have become more natural. Our parks and beaches are once again the peaceful retreats they were meant to be. Schools resume in a curious way and governments reassemble. New restrictions set in place this month are a striking reality. Bubbles are tightening and it feels like we are going to be here for a while.

January 1, 2021: New Year's intentions
This New Year's Day could not be more different than last, but with each new year I am left with learnings. Being curious about change, and seeing where my intentions land, is what carries me through. The changes that are hard to let go of, live on in my heart. I sit by the fire, flipping through my year in photos, contemplating a new screensaver. Inspiration trickles in. A sparkle from a tiny stone in my "Isla" ring catches my eye. I sparkle back, feeling the familiar crush in my heart and wonder what this new year will bring.

HOLDING ON

Wendy Wilkins Winslow

From our privileged perch on the western flank of the Caulfeild Plateau, I stare out past Bowen Island to the Salish Sea and beyond. It is a wet, dark December day. The sea is churning like my stomach as I contemplate what new disaster might befall us before this annus horribilis ends.

Here we are, a pandemic pod of two, my beautiful husband and I. When I married this Englishman he was tall, strong and adventurous. We lived and worked internationally and travelled the world. Today our world has shrunk. My husband has shrunk. Now we stay home. COVID-19 is only partially to blame.

In 2012, Rob was diagnosed with an aggressive prostate cancer. Since then he has had hormone therapy and radiation and more recently he was on an international research trial. It all took a huge toll on his aging body. There were no more sailing adventures to the Galapagos or hikes up Cypress Mountain. Even our usual walk along the seawall became too difficult. He was pale and breathless just climbing a flight of stairs, but he remained optimistic and for a while the treatments kept the cancer at bay.

In 2019, we took what would become our last trip. We flew to Boston for a boisterous, busy, happy family Christmas with my son and his family. Then we flew down the eastern seaboard to Marco Island for a week of Florida sunshine. While I went biking with grandchildren and deep sea fishing with my brother, Rob stayed behind in an easy chair. He watched TV, read, snoozed and proselytized about the downfall of the United States, often with his favourite single malt scotch in hand.

In early 2020, we came home to bad news. The cancer had not only spread, it had shifted into overdrive. Rob was admitted to hospital for further investigations. While his urologist was able to get him a same-day appointment with an oncologist, the hospital was unable to arrange transportation. So our new journey began by walking five blocks from the hospital to the Cancer Agency. When Rob was admitted I had taken his clothes home to wash. So, dressed in hospital pyjamas, with a blue gown tied at the back and his leather jacket on top, we shuffled down the hill. He also had two newly-acquired tubes poking into his kidneys with large urine bags attached. As we walked the bags flapped in the winter winds around his six foot, four inch frame. Looking around, I fervently hoped we wouldn't see anyone we knew. It was a long, painful five blocks.

The oncologist was not encouraging. "We can try chemotherapy, but I need to be clear, it is palliative, not curative."

Rob pushed him for an answer to the big question. "How long do I have?"

With the proviso, "I do not have a crystal ball," the oncologist allowed, "You have weeks becoming months, not months becoming years."

We clung to each other as we trudged slowly along the slushy sidewalks back to the hospital. Rob collapsed, shivering, into his much too short hospital bed. I pulled the faded yellow curtain closed and leaned in to wrap my arms around him. We sobbed convulsively.

Chemo did not go well. Rob was sick and severely immunocompromised. He ended up in the ER several times with rip-roaring infections. On one visit in April, Rob became a BC statistic: he caught COVID-19. Thirteen patients at Lions Gate Hospital caught COVID-19. Nine died.

I was a registered nurse for 50 years. Although I had not done clinical work for many years, I had learned a lot about prostate cancer in recent years. I learned how to manage PICC lines and pumps, antibiotics and analgesics. I learned how to do nephrostomy dressings and assist with physio exercises. I used my nursing knowledge and skill to help Rob make decisions, to care for him and to keep him safe. I couldn't protect him from COVID-19, but I could take him home and look after him there.

Rob coughed night and day. He ached all over. His heart raced to 140. His fever spiked to 39 and then he had massive sweats. I had to change the bedding again and again. His legs were swollen and turned blue. He couldn't move in bed and the skin on his bottom began to break down. When I did manage to get him up, he fainted. It was only months later that I realized I also had caught COVID-19. At the time I was too distracted to notice. I attributed the headaches, coughing and heart palpitations to stress. It was the worst of times.

It's a good thing we enjoy each other's company as we were in quarantine for the entire month of May. One evening after Rob had fallen asleep, I crept into bed beside him with a glass of wine and my iPad. I had helped him bathe. I had done dishes and housework and endless loads of laundry. I had cooked foods to entice him to eat. I had disassembled, unclogged and reassembled the drain under the kitchen sink. I suddenly realized I was doing everything I usually do, everything Rob usually did and everything our cleaning people usually did. I was shattered and exhausted beyond belief. I had become a leaky old bag. I cried if you just looked at me sideways.

I snuggled under the duvet hoping to take a few minutes to catch up on emails. As I was plumping the pillows I somehow managed to fling my glass across the bedroom. Red wine splattered all over the bedside table, the pale carpet and the faded green love seat. With my last ounce of strength I got up, scrubbed everything clean then crawled back into bed and wept.

Summer approached. As if cancer and COVID-19 were not enough of a challenge, Rob noticed that his eyesight was not so acute. "I need new glasses," he said. "The TV has gone all fuzzy. And I can't focus on this newspaper."

The optician misdiagnosed cataracts. After weeks of Rob's eyesight continuing to decline, we flung ourselves at the mercy of the ophthalmologist's front desk clerk and got an urgent appointment. The ophthalmologist sent him directly to the ER. After a CT, an MRI and endless hours in the hospital's draughty back corridors, the neurosurgeon announced that it was a large pituitary tumour, pressing on Rob's optic nerve, that was causing progressive blindness. "And I'm sorry to tell you it is inoperable, although radiation might be a possibility to slow its progress."

With radiation Rob's vision improved slightly, enough to watch TV and read large print. On October 27, he reached his goal of turning eighty. We celebrated him with five different parties. According to his wishes, each party involved a phenomenally rich chocolate ganache cake. Any additional time after eighty is the icing on my cake. In the meantime, Rob announced a new goal. "I want to live long enough to see Trump escorted out of the White House in January."

We both know what is next. We just don't know when. After much deliberation, Rob applied for medical assistance in dying. If and when the burden of living becomes too great, he has that option.

I hate seeing my sweet husband become a shadow of his former self: struggling to go up a few stairs, weeping in frustration that he can't drive or read or dress himself or do anything to help me. Why does it have to be so hard? We ask ourselves what we have done to deserve all of this. But it's a silly question. The answer is clear: old age is not for sissies.

Even with our world tilting sideways, I understand how fortunate I am to have had so many happy years with Rob. We sit close to each other in our small pandemic pod, away from the rest of the world. We hold hands. From our perch we watch the wind and rain swirling around our garden, the tall fir trees swaying and the whitecaps racing across the sea beyond. We talk about what the future holds. We cry. I read to him. During the day it is often Opinions from the *Globe and Mail*; at bedtime, it is Stephen Leacock or Stuart McLean. I have not abandoned my attempts to educate him about Canadian culture. He has not given up being engaged in the world.

We watch entirely too much TV, many of the classics like *Out of Africa*. I take him on a drive to see the twinkling Christmas lights people have put up especially early this year. They brighten all our worlds but he wants to come home after twenty minutes. At night I snuggle up close to him. He is warm and velvety and it helps me fall asleep.

"I want us to stay like this forever," I whisper.

But, in the light of day, we know we can't. So we savour each precious moment knowing that all we have is today and, if we are lucky, tomorrow. Perhaps we will have one last Christmas.

ABOUT THE WRITERS

ANNE BAIRD

Born in Borneo, Anne Baird is a West Vancouver artist and writer. She is a freelance journalist, has published 16 children's books, and writes and illustrates a small column, Anne's Corner, for The *Beacon*, about life in the slow lane. She is inspired by her three children, five grandchildren, and one great-grandchild. Also, by her mother, Ruth, and her seagull family, Busby, Mrs. Busby, and Busby Junior and the hummingbirds. Catch up with Anne at www.littlebigbooks.net.

ANNIE HILL

Annie Hill was born and raised in West Vancouver, where she continues to live with her husband, three teenaged children and two entertaining cats. After studying exercise physiology and healthy aging at UBC, she went on to work and teach at the University of Texas. Annie currently works as a health and fitness trainer for seniors. In her spare time, when she's not driving kids to and from activities, or cheering from the soccer sidelines, she can be found on the trails, up the mountains, at the beach or on the water – and almost always with family and friends.

BRENDA MORRISON

Brenda Morrison grew up wandering the hillside and seaside of West Vancouver. Her heart sang a deep song when her adventurous spirit brought her home, to raise her children, Hamish and Anna, close to the land and the family she holds dear. Her life's work is centred on respectful relationships with the land and its people, upholding the spirit of diversity and inclusion. She is honoured and grateful to be the Director of SFU's Centre for Restorative Justice and serve on the board of North Shore Restorative Justice. She believes *walking the talk* in your own backyard brings justice home.

CHRIS STRINGER

Chris Stringer has a passion for creativity. He considers himself the original fool rushing in where angels fear to tread – his explanation for launching the *Beacon* newspaper, with no experience in publishing or writing. His entrepreneurial business life has taken him across Canada and the US. Since retiring in West Vancouver, he has been a committed community volunteer, convinced that if he makes it to heaven it will be as a volunteer. He derives his strength and inspiration from his family who share him begrudgingly with his community hobbies.

DEANNA REGAN

Deanna Regan lives in Ambleside with her family and super dog, despite declaring loudly she would never be a dog owner. Preferring trail over asphalt, two wheels over four, wine over water, and wrinkles over Botox, she embraces life, change and writing in equal measure, cooking with waning enthusiasm, and has learned to never say never.

D.HIGGINS

D. Higgins is an Eagle Harbour citizen, swimmer and paddle-boarder. When she is not teaching, she observes the Parthenon eagles from land or water. Favourite times are spent in the company of her family, gardening or eating.

DOMENICA MASTROMATTEO

Domenica Mastromatteo lives in West Vancouver with her three children, two cats and her dog, Bonnie. She is currently completing a diploma from the Vancouver Art Therapy Institute. Domenica has worked with a wide range of clients (children, adolescents and adults) with a range of issues: PTSD, trauma, bereavement, ADHD, depression, anxiety and addictions. Her work with sensationalchildren.ca has assisted many families. She brings an understanding of the therapeutic process, fine arts, education and advocacy to her career as art therapist. Her eclectic artistic endeavours are documented at domenicamastromatteo.com.

ELIZABETH WOODING

Elizabeth has been living in West Vancouver with her family since 2004. She loves the outdoors and art in every form. She's come late to the art of writing and is discovering that it's in tense: it can happen in the past, present and future.

ELKE BABICKI

Elke Babicki, M.Ed., R.C.C. has been a consultant and clinical counsellor in Toronto and Vancouver for over thirty years. Her workshops and sessions in Europe and Canada have helped thousands of people claim more power in their lives. In 2011, Elke received the Women of Worth Leader of the Year Award for her work in supporting and inspiring women across the globe. She lives by the ocean in West Vancouver with her husband, Matt, an engineer and inventor. Her book, *Identity: From Holocaust to Hope,* was published in Germany as *Uebern Ozean* in 2017 with great success. For more on Elke go to www.elkebabicki.com.

FAY MEHR

Fay Mehr has been living in Canada since 1995. After settling in Vancouver, she started a career in sales and pursued a diploma in public relations. She currently works in the movie industry. Fay is passionate about psychology. She has taken many self-development classes over the years and hopes to pursue her psychology aspirations in the future. Fay enjoys a vibrant life in Vancouver with her friends and family and takes pleasure in reading, writing, traveling and recently, painting.

JENNIFER (LUTES) HILL
Jennifer is a bred, if not born, Vancouverite. In 1999 she crossed Lions Gate Bridge to start her family in West Vancouver. She is a mother to three daughters and an old dog. She lives in a little cottage by the sea and swims almost every day from June to October. Jennifer is passionate about health and wellness, writing and her daughters. Instagram: jenhill1228

JOANNE SINGLETON
Joanne has been a part of West Vancouver for over half a century, visiting her grandparents as a young girl and returning in her early 20s and again in 2006 with her family. She is an international Amazon bestselling author, and has had long-standing careers in both the legal and real estate professions. Joanne has treasured memories of West Vancouver and cherishes her walks with family through Memorial Park, Lighthouse Park, Ambleside and the spectacular seawall. She loves to travel and share a fine meal with those close to her heart. Joanne can be found at www.joannesingleton.com

JULIE FLYNN
Julie Flynn was born and raised in Newcastle, England. After a brief visit to Canada, she immigrated and made

North Vancouver her home in 2001. She soon developed a love for the great outdoors, especially trail running in the mountains. Julie's writing is inspired by her frequent adventures in the North Shore mountains and beyond. Her debut children's book, *Finn and the Magic Backpack*, was a #1 Amazon bestseller and a finalist in the 2018 Canadian Book Club Awards. She can be found at instagram.com/julieflynnwrites

KAREN HOFFMAN
Karen has lived in a creaky wood home in West Vancouver since 1990. When not staring at the stunning view, she holds company with friends or her two loving adult children. Her career began in finance and moved to social work where she facilitated circles of support for parents and kindergartners and taught SEL with North Shore Family Services. In retirement, Karen produces memory books for those who wish to preserve their legacy. She compiles stories and photos to create unique storybooks for family and friends to enjoy. Visit her website at www.moondancestories.com.

KAREN TIDBALL
The youngest of seven children, Karen Tidball is a migrant from a small farm in rural Saskatchewan. She has lived in West Vancouver since 2003. Mother to two daughters and a son, they, along with her husband, are the loves of her life. Karen enjoys swimming, hiking and exploring the world. She credits surviving non-Hodgkin's lymphoma in her twenties for helping to re-shape her life. Dedicated to

discovery, lifelong learning and a career of service to others, Karen is a Certified Professional Coach, committed to helping people lead careers and lives that satisfy them. linkedin.com/in/karen-tidball

KIMBERLEY CLARKE

Kimberley Clarke is a secondary school teacher of writing and literature as well as a poet, playwright and performer. She has been an educator forever and loves to learn and teach. She is the author of four and a half YA novels in *The Addie Sinclair Series*. The webpage for the series can be found under "The Addie Sinclair Series" and the books in the series can be found on Amazon or ordered wherever fine books can be ordered.

LINDY HUGHES PFEIL

For the past 20 years, Lindy has lived in a little blue cottage in Eagle Harbour. She collects rocks, loves tutus and the moon and walks barefoot whenever she can, even though it embarrasses her family. She believes world peace is entirely possible, if everyone would just write a book. So that's what she does – helps people write books. Like this one. And her greatest thrill is uncovering the magic in their stories. You can find her overfeeding the squirrels and jays on her deck, traipsing along Marine Drive, or online at lindypfeil.com.

L.NOËL

Laurisse spends her time flitting around what some call Vancouver in her tiny car. She is happiest with sand between her toes, salt water in her hair and a sour beer in hand. She is grateful to exist on the unceded lands of the Musqueam, Squamish and Tsleil-Waututh peoples.

MELODY NOBLE

Melody lives on the West Coast with her devoted husband and rowdy children. She grew up in rural Alaska with her identical twin sister, Harmony. Before becoming a writer, she was a nurse, owned and operated two coffee shops, and earned three science degrees. When not writing or trying to conceive, she can be found in nature, hunting, hiking, skiing, sailing or berry picking. She is socially aggressive and will befriend you while pumping gas then steal your name for her story's protagonist. Visit her online at melodynoble.wordpress.com

ROSE LEPIN

Sixteen-year-old Rose Lepin has been a resident of West Vancouver since she was two years old. Currently a grade 11 student, she is adjusting to the dynamic approach to schooling brought on by the pandemic. Rose is the current reigning Miss Teen Greater Vancouver (2019-2021) and a top 6 national finalist for Miss Teen Canada 2020. A *Beacon* contributor since grade 8, Rose hopes to use her voice to help others feel less alone. You can subscribe to Rose's blog, "Rose Lepin's Map of Madness" on mapofmadness.home.blog or follow her on Instagram at @roseofvancouver.

SHARON SELBY

Sharon Selby is a long-time resident of West Vancouver, where she lives with her husband, daughter and son. A Registered Clinical Counsellor, she has been supporting children, teens and families for the past 23 years, particularly in the area of anxiety. She is the author of a children's book on anxiety, *Surfing the Worry Imp's Wave*, and the recipient of the 2020 YWCA Metro Vancouver Woman of Distinction Award for the category of Connecting the Community. Her free ebook, *8 Common Mistakes to Avoid When Your Child Is Anxious*, is available at www.sharonselby.com/free.

SHARON THOMPSON

Sharon's 35 years in West Vancouver has been filled with family and friends; volunteering with colleagues and acquaintances; caring about neighbours and community. Many years of participating in school and neighborhood initiatives exposed her to countless volunteers and grew her sense of community. Stepping into provincial and municipal governance has unveiled a deep understanding and appreciation for the unparalleled breadth of local brain trust, talent and resourcefulness. She is ever inspired, grateful and proud to be a part of West Vancouver.

WENDY WILKINS WINSLOW

Wendy Winslow has lived in West Van for 50 of her 74 years. She has lived and worked internationally but is inevitably lured back to beautiful BC. Her husband, children and grandchildren have given her the love and strength to get through the year of COVID-19, her annus horribilis. Friends, Zoom yoga and chocolate have also helped.

Manufactured by Amazon.ca
Bolton, ON

18400193R00072